RUNNING ON EMPTY

SLEEPLESSNESS IN AMERICAN TEENS

CONNIE GOLDSMITH

TWENTY-FIRST CENTURY BOOKS / MINNEAPOLIS

Dedicated to the sleep specialists and other health care providers who work to improve America's sleep

Twenty-First Century Books™
An imprint of Lerner Publishing Group, Inc.
241 First Avenue North
Minneapolis, MN 55401 USA

For reading levels and more information, look up this title at www.lernerbooks.com.

Main body text set in Avenir.
Typeface provided by Linotype AG.

Library of Congress Cataloging-in-Publication Data

Names: Goldsmith, Connie, 1945– author.
Title: Running on empty : sleeplessness in American teens / Connie Goldsmith.
Description: Minneapolis : Twenty-First Century Books , [2021] | Includes bibliographical references and index. | Audience: Ages 11–18 | Audience: Grades 7–9 | Summary: "Young adults are one of the populations most impacted by poor sleep. Running on Empty provides a scientific and informative take on sleep and the impacts it has on stress levels, academic performance, and physical and mental health"— Provided by publisher.
Identifiers: LCCN 2020035530 (print) | LCCN 2020035531 (ebook) | ISBN 9781728415765 (library binding) | ISBN 9781728419107 (ebook)
Subjects: LCSH: Sleep disorders in adolescence—Juvenile literature.
Classification: LCC RJ506.S55 G66 2021 (print) | LCC RJ506.S55 (ebook) | DDC 618.92/8498—dc23

LC record available at https://lccn.loc.gov/2020035530
LC ebook record available at https://lccn.loc.gov/2020035531

Manufactured in the United States of America
1-48716-49126-10/9/2020

TABLE OF CONTENTS

**all human beings spend
1/3 of their lives asleep**

In physics class last year our professor talked about how dark energy
is still a transient concept, something that scientists everywhere
have yet to solidify with proof and consensus. And then one girl
in the class raised her hand and said that we spend one-third
of our lives asleep, *so why should it matter whether dark energy exists
or how the universe was formed anyway?*
And I thought about my grandfather eating his cereal alone every morning,
because he's so used to having it while my grandmother ate her eggs
that he can no longer get rid of the routine;
it's ingrained inside his bones like DNA.
I hope that if the universe ever does end, and if dark energy
has something to do with it, then what I had on this earth
was a good life, and maybe the two-thirds of it I spent with you
weren't so bad after all.

—*Meggie Royer,* Writings for Winter *blog, 2013*

4

CHAPTER 1
Are You Underslept?

Our sleeping time is as valuable a commodity as the time we are awake. Getting the right amount of sleep enhances the quality of every minute we spend with our eyes open.

—*Arianna Huffington, author and journalist, 2017*

Did you wake up tired and grumpy this morning? Barely make it to school? Fall asleep during fifth period? If so, you might be underslept. That means you didn't get as much sleep as you need, and you're walking around feeling really tired. You're not alone. Each night millions of Americans also experience sleep deprivation. They have trouble falling asleep or staying asleep. Lack of sleep affects teens even more than it affects adults because teens actually require more hours of sleep than adults do. Without adequate sleep, more than one-fourth of teens say they've fallen asleep at school. Lack of sleep can affect school and social life and can lead to unsafe driving practices.

A Public Health Epidemic

The Centers for Disease Control and Prevention (CDC), the US government organization responsible for monitoring health, considers sleep disorders such as insomnia a public health epidemic because they affect so many Americans. Insomnia is a sleep disorder characterized by an inability to get enough sleep. Insomnia can lead to sleep deprivation, but sleep deprivation can also be caused by choices a person makes, such as staying up late studying for a test. When you do that, you don't necessarily have insomnia, but you are sleep deprived.

Sleep deprivation can lead to poor performance during the day, especially at school or work. Inadequate sleep for any reason also leads to mental health issues such as anxiety, depression, and stress. And for a few people, not getting enough sleep can be downright dangerous. People may have serious car accidents if they drive while drowsy. Just like driving while drunk, drowsiness slows reaction time and leads to poor decision-making on the road. The National Safety Council estimates that drivers under the age of twenty-five are involved in at least 50 percent of the estimated six thousand fatal crashes each year related to drowsy driving.

Lack of sleep can lead to medical issues such as heart problems, diabetes, obesity, and high blood pressure. Insufficient sleep is suspected of being an early sign of Alzheimer's disease—a brain disease that leads to memory loss and dementia that is ultimately fatal. Sleep deprivation can even cause sleepwalking with fatal consequences, such as driving a car off a bridge or falling down the stairs.

We all need to make sleep a priority in our lives according to Dr. Timothy Morgenthaler, a past president of the American Academy of Sleep Medicine. "Healthy sleep is essential for physical health, mental well-being, and personal and public safety," he said. "Sleep is a necessity, not a luxury, and the promotion of healthy sleep should be a fundamental public health priority."

HOW LONG SHOULD YOU SLEEP?

The National Sleep Foundation recommends the following amount of daily sleep for various age groups.

1. Newborns (birth to 3 months old): 14 to 17 hours
2. Infants (4 to 11 months old): 12 to 15 hours
3. Toddlers (1 to 2 years old): 11 to 14 hours
4. Preschoolers (3 to 5 years old): 10 to 13 hours
5. School-age children (6 to 13 years old): 9 to 11 hours
6. Teenagers (14 to 17 years old): 8 to 10 hours
7. Young adults (18 to 25 years old): 7 to 9 hours
8. Adults (26 to 64 years old): 7 to 9 hours
9. Older adults (65 and older): 7 to 8 hours

Symptoms of Insomnia among Adolescents

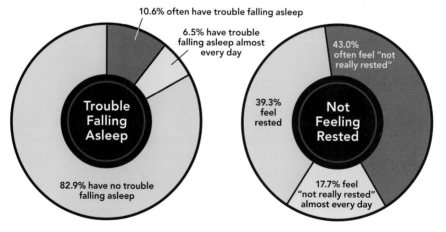

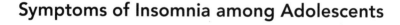

While most teens have no trouble falling asleep, just over 60 percent feel they are not really rested some or most days.

Lucretia King, a senior at Redwood High School in Larkspur, California, knows a lot about insomnia. She's suffered from it since the seventh grade and only manages to get four to five hours of sleep each night. She's tired most of the time, and her grades have slipped from As and Bs to Bs and Cs. When King spoke to her school newspaper for an article about insomnia, she said that she often can't remember names or memorize the information she needs to know for class. "It's very difficult [to stay focused in class]. I'll start thinking about things because I can't focus on the teachers," King says. "[Insomnia] makes me crankier than I should be at this age, and more irritated. I also don't have a big tolerance with people when they're annoying, which is a problem. I have a bad short term memory, which I believe comes from not sleeping."

The mission of the National Sleep Foundation, based in Arlington, Virginia, is to improve health through educating the public about the importance of sleep. Experts there say that adolescents should get eight to ten hours of sleep each night. Yet a poll of twelfth graders found that three-fourths of them slept fewer than eight hours per night, while half slept only seven hours or less. Like King, teens with insomnia say they have trouble falling sleep, and they're tired when they wake up. Some teens have problems every day with sleep, while others experience insomnia less often.

> **"I think sleeping was my problem in school.**
> **If school had started at four in the afternoon,**
> **I'd be a college graduate today."**
>
> *—George Foreman, former American heavyweight*
> *champion boxer who competed between*
> *1969 and 1997*

ARE YOU A NIGHT OWL OR A MORNING LARK?

Humans have a natural internal clock that makes them sleepy after a long day and wakes them after sleep. But different people have different sleep-wake cycles.

Night owls. About three out of ten people are night owls. Night owls don't feel tired until late in the evening and often prefer to stay up until midnight or even later. It can be hard for a night owl to get up early in the morning. Often being a night owl is not a choice. It may be genetic. In general, Western societies are most active in the daytime, especially during school and work hours. Night owls usually have to adjust, even though they are not naturally bright and bushy-tailed at 6:00 a.m.

Morning larks. About four out of ten people are morning larks. They go to bed early and get up early. They have plenty of energy in the morning and are ready to tackle the day ahead, whether it's school or work. The sleep-wake rhythm of most societies tends to favor larks, who may perform better at school or work in the morning than owls do.

Lydia M. Wytrzes, MD, is a sleep medicine specialist in private practice in Sacramento, California. She says chronic sleep deprivation is the most serious sleep-related issue that teens face. "This is aggravated by two biologically-driven changes in the teenage years. First, the sleep "clock" shifts so that sleep onset is delayed. Teens become natural "night owls" because of this. And the need for sleep actually increases in these years, perhaps due to hormonal changes. Coupled with early school start times, evening activities, and electronic devices that interfere with ideal bedtime routines, many teens don't get enough sleep."

The brain needs nutrition as much as the body does, and sleep is food for the brain. Getting enough sleep promotes mental alertness and physical healing. It also leads to improved athletic and school performance. Why do little kids fall asleep so easily when it's so difficult for so many teens? Getting the right amount of sleep can seem like a mystery. Scientists are working to learn more about how and why we sleep.

Even Fruit Flies Need to Sleep

Several groups of researchers have studied fruit fly sleep behavior. It turns out that people and fruit flies have a lot in common when it comes to sleep. Like people, the flies sleep at night and may take afternoon naps. If they're tired, they perform poorly on memory tests. And just as people who drink coffee stay more alert, caffeine keeps fruit flies awake as well. Experiments show that nerves in fruit fly brains help control their sleep in a similar way that human brains control human sleep.

Insufficient sleep among teens often negatively impacts academic performance. With online learning during the coronavirus pandemic, many students were spending eight to ten hours more online each day than they did prior to the virus. As a result, experts say it's even more important to turn off devices a couple hours before bedtime to allow the brain and body to calm down for a good night's sleep.

WORLD SLEEP DAY

The World Sleep Society organizes World Sleep Day, an annual event on the Friday before the spring equinox, the date in March when the sun crosses the equator, signaling the beginning of spring. The purpose of the event is to raise awareness of the importance of sleep and to decrease sleep problems through prevention and healthy management of sleep disorders.

Researchers and doctors from around the world participate in World Sleep Day in events and activities that promote the importance of healthy sleep. Sleep specialists discuss the newest research about ways to improve sleep health and to prevent and treat sleep disorders.

Researchers at Harvard University in Massachusetts are studying the genes of underslept fruit flies. The scientists hope one day to use the genetic information they discover about fruit fly sleep to improve human sleep. For example, one study showed that sleep deprivation in young flies impacts their brain development. Scientists think this suggests that sleep for young people is critical for proper brain development.

Teens and Devices

Sixteen-year-old Jesse Smith feels under pressure. "I think social media and excessive amounts of homework prevent teens from getting the amount of sleep they need," he says. "I only get about six hours of sleep each night. I use my electronic devices late into the evening, but I do turn my phone off about forty-five minutes before I plan on going to sleep," he says.

Research has shown that the light from electronic devices interferes with some of the brain chemistry that assists sleep. The light upsets the body's natural internal clock, which guides us to wake up in the morning and fall asleep at night. Light from

Teen Time on Social Media

Hours per day	Boys (%)	Girls (%)
Less than one hour	43.8	22.8
Between one and three hours	32.1	31.1
From three to five hours	10.4	17.7
More than five hours	13.7	28.4

electronic devices before bedtime gets in the way of everyone's ability to fall asleep easily and leads to insomnia. But it affects teens more than other age groups. Experts at the National Sleep Foundation recommend restricting the use of devices near bedtime. The foundation's website suggests, "Try setting the [device] curfew at two hours before bed, one hour before bed, or even thirty minutes before bed—the earlier in the evening, the better, but whatever feels realistic."

Studies show that many teens spend too much time on social media activities in the United States and in other countries as well. The prestigious British Broadcasting Corporation (BCC) studied a group of twelve thousand British teens who routinely use social media in the evening on a typical school day. The BBC researchers found that teens who use social media for more than three hours a day are more likely to go to bed after 11:00 p.m. and to wake during the night. One in five teens spends five hours or more on social media each day.

CHAPTER 2

Over the Edge

Two years tomorrow. Heart/being/soul/identity/ motherdom/existence/universe shattered in an eye's blink. No warning. No sense. No fair. Miss him with every heartbeat, every breath, always and endless.

—Susan Wood, 2019, about the death of her teen son in 2017

Susan Wood woke up early on Memorial Day in 2017. She fed the dog and headed into the kitchen to make a cup of tea. She planned to let her fourteen-year-old daughter and sixteen-year-old son Dalton sleep as late as they wanted. Dalton was especially tired after a full week of school and his first week at a new job at a supermarket in Norfolk, Virginia.

Wood glanced out the window and saw a police car parked in front of her house. Two officers got out of the car and walked along the brick path toward the door. "I wondered if there had been some kind of vandalism nearby and if the police were checking with the neighbors for any leads. I opened the door before they even knocked, ready to help if I could."

But they weren't looking for leads—they were looking for Wood. "One officer asked if I was related to Dalton. 'Yes, he's my son,' I answered, bewildered. What could they want with him? The other officer said, 'There's been an accident, and you need to get to the hospital immediately.' That's all they would tell me.

"The next twenty minutes unspooled in surreal slow motion," Wood remembers. "Dashing up the stairs to throw on some clothes, shocked to see Dalton's empty bed. Racing to the hospital a few minutes away, heart banging in my ears, speeding through yellow lights with the cops blowing through red lights with blaring sirens as they followed right behind me. Bursting through the emergency room doors and being quickly ushered into a tiny room away from the main waiting area. A white-coated doctor with a clipboard murmuring, 'I'm very sorry. We did everything we could.'

"Calling my parents, struggling to choke out two simple words: Dalton's dead." Wood had kissed her son good night fewer than eight hours before his death. After her parents arrived at the hospital, they went to her house and woke Dalton's sister. "They told her Dalton was dead and brought her to the hospital to be with me. Like all of us, my daughter was stunned and in a state of shock." Dalton's dad was out of town but quickly returned when he got the news.

Searching for a Cause

"The next twenty-four hours were a blur," Wood said. "Detectives searched every inch of Dalton's room; they took his phone, laptop, and backpack to the police lab for analysis. The lead detective interviewed Dalton's friends. Even though the police found no evidence of substance abuse, depression, bullying, emotional distress of any kind, no suicide note or anything to suggest Dalton had been thinking about suicide, the cops said Dalton's death was a suicide. The medical examiner agreed."

Over the next few days, and with the help of the police, eyewitnesses, and a review of surveillance footage, Wood and her family pieced together what had happened to Dalton. "Around 5 a.m. that Memorial Day morning, Dalton left his bed," Wood said. "He didn't put on his glasses, even though he was so nearsighted he never went anywhere without them. Dressed in the old T-shirt and shorts that he slept in, he left the house without his cell phone but carried his heavy school backpack, which he hated."

Dalton walked nearly 2 miles (3.2 km) in his stocking feet to the parking garage of Old Dominion University in Norfolk and climbed to the top of the five-story structure. The garage was a hangout for Dalton and his friends because it had a great view of the school's football stadium. At the same time, two skateboarders—planning to use the empty parking garage ramps for skateboard practice—stepped from the elevator. They spotted Dalton at the edge of the parking deck and shouted to him.

When Dalton's grandmother later reviewed the security footage captured by cameras in the garage, she saw what happened next. "When the boys shouted, Dalton appeared startled and confused. He dropped his backpack, scrambled over the deck's low retaining wall, and plunged five stories to the ground." One of the skateboarders called 911 at 6:13 a.m. Paramedics arrived quickly and took Dalton to the nearest hospital emergency room. Doctors pronounced him dead at 6:44 a.m., fourteen minutes before his mother arrived at the hospital.

Breaking an "Already Shattered Heart"

Although the police and medical examiner ruled Dalton's death a suicide, Susan Wood never believed it. "It made no sense," she said. "This was a smart, logical, practical kid. In my heart, in my gut, I knew this was no suicide. And I wasn't the only one to doubt that Dalton had taken his own life. When I visited his principal the next morning to let her know why Dalton wouldn't be returning to school, she wondered if he had been sleepwalking." She remembered a young man in her hometown who sometimes woke up in other people's houses without having any idea how he got there. Dalton's teachers and friends also suspected sleepwalking because no one who knew Dalton had ever seen any behavior that would explain a death from suicide.

"Dalton was an awesome kid and an honor-roll student in his high school's engineering and leadership program," Wood said. "Friends and teachers alike adored him. He tutored struggling students; he befriended and advocated for LGBTQ, autistic, and marginalized teens at his school. He'd just turned in his course requests for the fall and was looking forward to AP classes with some of his favorite teachers, as well as heading up the shop crew for the school's robotics team. Dalton had just landed his first job and would get his driver's license over the summer. He had everything going for him."

It took Wood several months to decide if she wanted to contest the medical examiner's ruling of suicide on Dalton's death certificate. "It wouldn't bring him back, so did it really matter? I was submerged in grief, the sorrow of my loss so intense I could sometimes barely breathe. Did I have the emotional strength to do anything more than keep myself semi-together for my daughter? But what was recorded on the death certificate, what was written into history, was an untruth. And as the days rolled on, I knew I needed to advocate for my son."

As a writer, Wood was skilled at conducting research and speaking with experts. She reviewed the academic and medical literature about sleepwalking. "I learned of non-REM parasomnia [a state of semiconsciousness that occurs in stages of sleep other than the rapid eye movement, or REM, stage] in which people, trapped between a sleep and waking state, can perform all sorts of activities—cook, jog, drive, even commit violent crimes or harm themselves—without knowing what they're doing. During these events, the brain is awake enough to perform complex motor and verbal functions, but is asleep enough so people don't have awareness of, or responsibility for, their actions."

The literature warned that startling people in such a state can confuse and disorient them. When the boys called out to Dalton in the parking garage, that's exactly what happened. Deaths related to these kinds of sleepwalking events are often mischaracterized as suicides, Wood learned. "Sleepwalking? To your death? Unfathomable," she said. "What I discovered broke my already shattered heart."

In January 2018, Wood sent a lengthy and well-researched document to the state medical examiner explaining why Dalton's death should not be ruled a suicide. She wrote about parasomnia and sleepwalking. She described the events leading to Dalton's death and presented an overview of the legal definition of suicide. She attached copies of her correspondence with leading sleep specialists and included a copy of the article "Parasomnia Pseudo-Suicide" from a prominent medical journal.

Wood had consulted with medical and legal specialists about Dalton's case. They suspected a complex sleepwalking event. Dr. Michel A. Cramer Bornemann, then an expert in sleep disorders at Minnesota Regional Sleep Disorders Center in Minneapolis, wrote to Wood, "Though one will never know with certainty the degree of consciousness/awareness (or lack thereof) during the episode prior to your son's tragic death, my colleagues at Sleep Forensics Associates would suspect a complex sleepwalking event (or NREM Parasomnia) based upon the information that you provided to us."

Wood concluded her presentation to the medical examiner with this request: "In the absence of definitive, positive proof that Dalton's death was an intentional suicide, and in light of the significant and overwhelming evidence consistent with an accident during a non-REM parasomnia sleepwalking event, including the professional opinion of leading sleep pathology physician experts, we respectfully request that Dalton's manner of death be revised from suicide to accident or undetermined."

After the medical examiner had reviewed the documents, Wood spoke with her over the phone. "She seemed skeptical at first, but as we further discussed my research and the conclusions of the experts, she finally agreed that a fatal fall during a non-REM parasomnia event seemed to explain what happened to Dalton and that it was not an intentional suicide." The medical examiner changed the manner of death from suicide to undetermined, and Dalton's death certificate was amended with that wording.

"I'm finally at a point where I can share the complete story," Wood said. "Dalton's truth, my truth. I read in the news recently of a Pennsylvania kid who'd sleepwalked four miles [6.4 km] to his middle school carrying his backpack. I realized teens and parents need to know about this. What happened to Dalton can happen to any child. Lack of quality sleep can put kids at serious risk for dangerous, even deadly, parasomnias. I needed to tell young people about what happened to Dalton—all of it. For me and especially for him."

CHAPTER 3

The Science of Sleep

Sleep is not the absence of wakefulness. Our nighttime
sleep is an exquisitely complex, metabolically active,
and deliberately ordered series of unique states.
Numerous functions of the brain are restored by, and
depend upon, sleep.

—*Matthew Walker, professor of neuroscience and psychology
at the University of California, Berkeley, 2017*

Before the 1950s, scientists believed that the human brain and
body completely shut down for the night so we could recover
from the mental and physical stress of each day. But researchers
have since learned that sleep is far more complicated. It may seem
as if you and your brain go to bed, eventually fall asleep, and then
wake up. But now we know that when we sleep, our brains remain
as active as ever.

Sleeping in Stages

The human brain cycles through several stages of sleep during the night. Three stages of sleep lead to rapid eye movement (REM) sleep. REM is the stage when the sleeper is often dreaming and the eyes flick back and forth as if the dreamer were watching a movie playing on the inside of the closed eyelids. The three stages of sleep are these:

- **Stage 1.** This is the transition from wakefulness to light sleep. Within ten minutes of lying down with the intention of going to sleep, heartbeat, breathing, and brain activity begin to slow. Muscle activity decreases. Sometimes people experience brief and sudden involuntary muscle contractions. They may jerk awake momentarily or feel as if they're falling in space. This is more likely to happen when people are very tired or anxious. It's easy to wake people in stage 1 sleep.
- **Stage 2.** During this stage, the heart and breathing slow even more, and the entire body relaxes. Together, stages 1 and 2 last about thirty minutes. Body temperature begins to drop in preparation for deeper sleep. Brain activity slows even further. People spend more of their sleeping time in stage 2 than in other stages. It's more difficult to wake people in stage 2 than in stage 1.
- **Stage 3.** The deep sleep we need to feel refreshed in the morning occurs during this stage. Most of our deep sleep occurs during the first half of the night. The electrical impulses in the brain slow down even more, as do breathing and heartbeat. Your muscles are very relaxed, and you don't wake up easily. During this sleep stage, your body does most of the hard work. It repairs and heals muscles, cleanses the cerebrospinal fluid that circulates through the brain and

spinal cord, stimulates growth, boosts energy for the next day, and works to keep you well by improving the function of your immune system. It can be very difficult to wake a person from stage 3.

- **REM sleep.** Stages 1 through 3 build to REM sleep, the time when most dreams occur. Many of us remember our dreams when we wake up. Other people forget them. But if you wake someone during REM sleep, they can most likely tell you what they're dreaming about at that moment. During REM sleep, the brain becomes more active, heart rate and blood pressure rise, and breathing becomes fast and irregular. One complete sleep cycle, which includes the first three stages and REM sleep, lasts about ninety to one hundred minutes. Most people experience four to five cycles per night. Several changes in the sleep cycle occur when people get older. Men, especially, take longer to fall asleep, may awaken more often during the night, and have less REM sleep.

An important feature of REM sleep is that arm and leg muscles become temporarily paralyzed, protecting and preventing the sleeper from acting out dreams. This is important because most of us have dreamed of being chased by crazed people or scary animals, or running from an impending disaster. If we could act out our dreams, the streets would be filled with sleeping people running amok like zombies!

On rare occasions, people do act out their dreams. In September 2019, twenty-nine-year-old Jenna Evans was having a vivid dream in which she and her fiancé were in a dangerous situation with bad guys on a high-speed train. "He [the fiancé] told me I had to swallow my [engagement] ring to protect it; so I popped that sucker off, put it in my mouth and swallowed it with a glass of water right about the time I realized what I was doing. I assumed this too was a dream, because WHO ACTUALLY SWALLOWS THEIR ENGAGEMENT RING, so I went back to sleep."

The next day, an X-ray clearly showed the ring in Evans's stomach. After one doctor removed it, another doctor suggested that Evans see a sleep specialist because she may have had an episode of REM sleep behavior disorder. This disorder leads to a variety of symptoms. For example, a person may not experience—at least part of the time—the paralysis that normally happens during REM sleep. This can lead people to act out their dreams, especially when dreams are intense or violent.

What Do Dreams Mean?

Dreams have fascinated people for centuries. Ancient Egyptians recorded dreams on papyrus, believing them to be revelations from the gods. Early Greeks and Romans believed dreams were predictions of future events or visits from the dead. In 1900 Austrian neurologist and psychoanalyst Sigmund Freud published the groundbreaking work *The Interpretation of Dreams*. He wrote that dreams help us unlock the unconscious mind and provide symbols of repressed fears and desires that may be too painful to experience directly. In the twenty-first century, psychoanalysts help patients analyze their dreams as part of the therapeutic experience.

Not all researchers agree with psychoanalysts such as Freud. For example, sleep medicine specialist Wytrzes says, "Dreams are not some deep manifestation of underlying conflict that can only come to light with sleep. What people consider dreams are story-like intervals that are most typically recalled during or following REM sleep. We dream continuously and in all stages of sleep, but dreams are more organized during REM sleep. They proceed in a fashion that can be remembered and reported back like a story." Why we dream and the function of REM sleep remains

Sigmund Freud's *The Interpretation of Dreams* was one of the most important contributions to psychoanalysis. Freud developed this method of understanding the interaction of the human mind's conscious and unconscious aspects. In his book about dreams, originally published in his native German, he analyzed his own dreams as well as hundreds of dreams from his patients.

controversial. Wytrzes's best guess? "REM sleep reinforces learned behavior. During dreams, new memories are slotted into pre-existing knowledge and the brain tries to make sense of it."

Are dreams secret codes into our inner lives? Some scientists say no. "What if there's no secret code, and we've been spending our time reading into a bunch of random images, much like people find shapes and objects hidden in the clouds?" David B. Feldman, counseling psychologist at Santa Clara University in California, asks, "What if dreams don't actually mean anything?"

Some scientists say dreams are a side effect of normal brain processes during sleep, a sort of neurological housecleaning. The brain is very active during sleep, triggering random sensations, emotions, and memories. "Our brains assemble all of this underlying activity into a story," according to Feldman. "But this story doesn't actually mean anything. It's simply an attempt to make sense of the neural activity that has taken place. This is why dreams seem so illogical and strange."

On the other hand, dreams can be an important source of creativity for many people. Dreams are important to Maggie Stiefvater, author of the best-selling teen series the Raven Cycle. In an interview with *Publishers Weekly* in 2019, she said, "I love dreaming. When I'm well, I dream every single night—crazy, lucid dreams. And I can always tell when I'm on the right track with a book: when I start to actually dream scenes of the book."

So what do dreams mean? Is it nothing, as Feldman suggests, or do they really mean something, as so many others believe? Google "what do dreams mean" and you'll come up with dozens of interpretations that you may or may not accept. What do your dreams mean to you? Are they trying to tell you something? The Lucid Dream Society suggests keeping dream journals to help you remember and control your dreams. "By simply writing in detail each morning the dreams that you had, in just a few weeks you will be able to see a huge difference in your dream recall!"

> **"I love sleep. My life has a tendency to fall apart when I'm awake, you know?"**
>
> —**Ernest Hemingway, American author (1899–1961)**

Must We Sleep?

Why do we sleep? Wouldn't you rather spend an extra hour or three with your friends instead? What do we get in return for giving up so much of our precious time to sleep? It turns out that sleep helps your body and your brain in many ways. "Sleep affects almost every tissue in our bodies," says Dr. Michael Twery, sleep expert from the National Institutes of Health based in Bethesda, Maryland. "It affects growth and stress hormones, our immune system, appetite, breathing, blood pressure, and cardiovascular health." Tired people are less effective at school and at work. "Loss of sleep impairs your higher levels of reasoning, problem-solving and attention to detail," neuroscientist and sleep expert Dr. Merrill

After winning five gold medals in Stuttgart, Germany, in 2019, Simone Biles became the most decorated gymnast of all time at world championships. To compete at the highest level, Biles makes sure to eat a healthy diet and to get a good night's sleep.

Mitler of the National Institutes of Health says. Tired people are at higher risk for traffic accidents than people who get enough sleep. According to Mitler, "Lack of sleep also influences your mood, which can affect how you interact with others. A sleep deficit over time can even put you at greater risk for developing depression."

Sleep restores energy and improves motor skills, so it's not surprising that some of the best athletes in the world are big fans of sleep. Sprinter and Olympic gold medal winner Usain Bolt says, "Sleep is extremely important to me—I need to rest and recover in order for the training I do to be absorbed by my body." When he was competing, Bolt slept up to ten hours every night and would often nap before his record-breaking sprints.

Gymnast and Olympic gold medal winner Simone Biles says, "Sleep is the #1 thing besides my eating habits. I'm always looking forward to sleep." It wasn't always that way. In the past, Biles didn't worry much about sleep. "I could stay up until 1:00 a.m., and have practice at 8:00 a.m. or 9:00 a.m. and then I'd be fine. Now if it's starting to creep around 9:00 p.m. or 10:00 p.m., I start panicking, and I'm having anxiety and I think I need to go to bed—it's my bedtime. I get a little bit delirious if I don't get a good night's sleep," she says.

Sleep Loss and Sports Injury

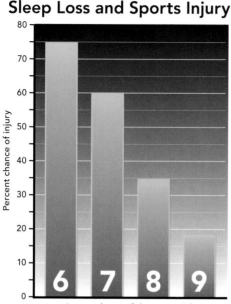

The chance of a sports injury falls dramatically as the hours of sleep per night increase. Teens who sleep only six hours each night have a 75 percent chance of sustaining a sports injury, while those sleeping eight hours have a 35 percent chance. Sleeping nine hours decreases the risk of a sports-related injury to less than 20 percent.

Not only does adequate sleep promote better physical performance, but it also reduces the risk of sports injuries. An athlete who sleeps only six hours has a much higher rate of injury than does the athlete who sleeps nine hours. A well-slept athlete is more focused and precise in their effort than an athlete who is trying to get by on insufficient sleep.

Sleep to Remember

Sleep helps us remember information. A structure in the human brain called the hippocampus is a short-term storage site for the names, faces, and facts a person takes in on any given day. But the hippocampus has limited storage capacity. If it gets too full, some memories are knocked aside to make room for others. That's where sleep comes in. When you sleep, your brain moves your memories from short-term to long-term storage. Sleep and learning are therefore closely linked. If you need a surefire way to improve your performance on an exam, study in the afternoon and then sleep well the night before.

Learning can even happen during sleep, and at any age. "Sleep learning, as I called it, worked for me in two ways. I took a typing class in high school to prepare me for college," said Karen Carson, a recently retired nurse. "I spent hours typing in my dreams, fingers on all the correct keys. Once in the classroom, it seemed that I learned to be a fast and accurate typist more quickly than many other students." Sleep learning also worked for Carson in nursing school. "When I took bacteriology, a lot of my dreams involved looking through a microscope and identifying dozens of different bacteria by their Latin names. I worked hard in my dreams, but it gave me an edge in my real-life studies."

Jeri Chase Ferris acts in plays in the Northern California retirement community where she lives. "There are times when I need to memorize up to eighty pages of lines for a play. I repeat lines from various scenes over and over as I'm going to sleep, and after a few weeks of nightly 'dream rehearsals' the entire play is firmly in my memory." Writers sometimes even compose stories or plots in their sleep! What have you learned in your sleep?

Sleep to Forget

Walker says that forgetting nonessential information also occurs during sleep. "Sleep seems to provide a form of forgetting. Sleep will enhance that which is necessary and important to remember. And it will actually let go of that which doesn't seem to be important to you."

Sleep clears up storage space in the brain and provides us with a clean start to each day, free of unnecessary facts and figures. Do you need to remember what you had for lunch last month or the name of every person you passed in the hall at school two days ago? Not really. Do you need to remember your locker combination and how to solve that algebra equation for the test tomorrow? Yes. And sleeping can help prioritize the information that you do need to hang on to.

Sleep to a Healthier You

Sleep does much more than improve your athletic performance and help you learn. It enhances problem-solving and decision-making skills. Sleep can make you more creative. It helps you control your emotions and behavior and improves your coping skills. Not getting enough sleep has been linked to depression and even thinking about or attempting suicide. Teens who don't get enough sleep may have problems getting along with others. They may act impulsively and get angry easily. Lack of sleep can lead to mood swings, poor motivation, and problems with school and grades, as well as with social interactions.

Getting enough sleep also decreases the risk of teen obesity in several ways, according to an article from the Harvard T. H. Chan School of Public Health:

- Sleep deprivation alters hormones that control hunger.
- Being awake longer gives people more time to eat.
- Tired people tend to get less exercise.
- Overall, sleepy people may choose less healthy diets.

Teens who get enough sleep tend to eat a better diet and have an overall healthier lifestyle. Teens who sleep less tend to crave late-night snacks because fatigue increases the desire for high-fat, high-sugar food. That often leads to unhealthy weight gain.

Scientists know that the brain sends out signals that control the body's hormones. Some of those hormones regulate appetite.

The hormone leptin makes us feel full. When the body releases it, we're likely to stop eating. But when the body releases the hormone ghrelin, it makes us want to eat more. Dr. Yaqoot Fatima, an epidemiologist at James Cook University in Australia, studies the link between sleep and body weight. She says, "Overall, sleep deprivation leads to an alteration in the levels of these hormones. That, in turn, affects the [body's] energy balance . . . and leads to weight gain."

Sleep helps regulate a number of other important hormones that repair cells and promote growth in young people. And the more sleep you get, the stronger your immune system becomes, which improves your chances of successfully fighting off infections. One study showed people who average fewer than seven hours of sleep each night are three times as likely to come down with a cold than those who get enough sleep.

Ticktock Goes Your Clock

Chemicals and hormones continually flow through the brain, helping to put us to sleep or to wake us up. During sleep, electrical impulses surge along the brain's nerve pathways, escorting us through the different stages of sleep. The brain helps us know when it's time to sleep and time to wake up by releasing chemical signals that cycle in a day-night rhythm. The rhythm makes us feel alert at one time (usually during the day) and sleepy at another time (usually at night).

Most living creatures have an internal clock to regulate the sleep-wake cycle over a twenty-four-hour period. The rotation of Earth creates the cycle of day and night, and our internal clock follows that pattern. According to Walker, "The light of the sun methodically resets our inaccurate internal timepiece each and every day, 'winding' us back to precisely, not approximately, twenty-four hours."

Scientists refer to this internal clock as the circadian rhythm. The circadian rhythm regulates not only sleep and wakefulness but also many other physical functions. These include body temperature, blood pressure, hunger, and activity and energy levels. The circadian rhythm even affects moods and emotions.

How does this rewinding occur? The internal clock resides deep inside the brain in the suprachiasmatic nucleus, or SCN. The SCN is where the optic nerves from our eyes meet and cross just below the middle of the brain. The SCN samples the light each optic nerve receives and uses it to calibrate our internal clock.

Circadian Rhythm

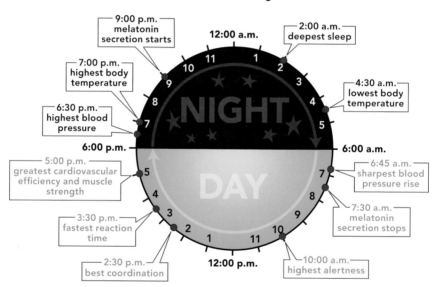

Many of our body's activities are determined by our circadian rhythm. For example, the brain begins releasing sleep-promoting melatonin at about 9:00 p.m. Typically, our deepest sleep occurs around 2:00 a.m. Melatonin secretion stops at 7:30 a.m., leading to the period of highest alertness around 10:00 a.m., which for most teens is during the school day. Coordination, reaction time, and muscle strength increase throughout the afternoon.

> "Humans are not sleeping the way nature intended. The number of sleep bouts, the duration of sleep, and when sleep occurs has all been . . . distorted by modernity."
>
> —Matthew Walker, professor of neuroscience and psychology at the University of California, Berkeley, 2017

With the Industrial Revolution of the nineteenth century, new factories began to produce everyday items in large quantities. The work schedule shifted dramatically away from the natural cycle of laboring during daylight hours and sleeping at night. By the twenty-first century, many people work at night and sleep during the day. In fact, nearly 20 percent of American workers are employed in shift work. This includes doctors and nurses, police and firefighters, members of the military, and people in transportation and food service. Some shift workers get used to working at night and sleeping during the day, but many don't. Fewer than two-thirds of shift workers report getting enough sleep. People who rotate shifts—moving from a daytime shift to a nighttime shift and back—have an especially difficult time adjusting.

Another challenge to our internal clock is the change to daylight savings time (DST) from standard time. The original idea behind DST was to push clocks an hour forward in the spring and an hour back in the fall to have additional daylight time and to conserve on energy for lighting. However, DST means our sleep pattern is off by an hour as the human body acclimates to the change. It can take anywhere from a couple of days or more for the circadian rhythm to adjust. Jet lag also disrupts the circadian rhythm as travelers move across geographical time zones, losing time (according to the clock) as they move eastward and gaining

The Brain and Sleep

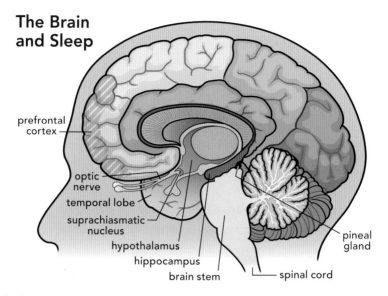

prefrontal
cortex

optic
nerve

temporal lobe

suprachiasmatic
nucleus

hypothalamus

hippocampus

brain stem

pineal
gland

spinal cord

The brain is part of regulating our human sleep patterns. For example, the suprachiasmatic nucleus is where optic nerves from our eyes meet and cross. It helps calibrate our internal clock. The pineal gland secretes melatonin when stimulated by the suprachiasmatic nucleus.

time as they move westward. For example, people who travel from the Pacific time zone in California to the eastern time zone in New York experience a loss of three hours. So when it is 9:00 p.m. in Los Angeles, it's midnight in New York City. Long flights, such as those to Australia, Asia, or Europe from the United States, involve losing or gaining as many as sixteen hours. It usually takes a few days for the body's circadian rhythm to adjust to the new time zone.

The Dracula Hormone

The multitasking SCN uses a hormone called melatonin to trigger the repeating cycle of sleep and wakefulness. When darkness falls—as perceived through the optic nerve—the SCN turns on the pineal gland, a pea-sized organ in the center of the brain.

In response, the pineal gland begins to release melatonin, also known as the Dracula hormone because the brain produces it only in the dark. The darker it gets, the more melatonin floods the brain. Melatonin doesn't actually put us to sleep. It regulates the timing of when we will feel sleepy.

The teen brain begins making melatonin later at night than the brains of children and adults. Many teens have to be at school early in the morning, so they often have trouble getting enough sleep the night before. They are not just being difficult when they stay up past midnight and struggle to make it through the next day at school. They naturally have more trouble falling asleep earlier in the evening and find it more difficult to wake early in the morning.

Specialized cells within the brain produce a chemical called gamma-aminobutyric acid, or GABA. This chemical helps the nervous system relax, reduces stress and pain, and suppresses activity in parts of the brain that normally arouse or waken us, thus boosting our drive to sleep. The brain activity and chemicals that make us sleepy and that awaken us work together to help us get the right amount of sleep at night while keeping us active the rest of the time.

COVID-19, ANXIETY, AND SLEEP

In late 2019, a new and deadly respiratory virus emerged in China. Known as SARS-CoV-2, the novel coronavirus and the disease it causes—COVID-19—swept around the globe. In late March 2020, as the global pandemic was worsening, the *New York Times* offered this tip to better sleeping during stressful times: limit media consumption in the evening. "Sleep is hard when anxiety levels are high," said Dr. Douglas B. Kirsch, neurologist and former president of the American Academy of Medicine. "Only look at coronavirus news once per day, preferably not near bedtime. We tend to keep our anxieties bottled up and they burst out in the dark." Try to use the time before bed to put away fears, perhaps by meditation or other relaxing activities.

Blue Light and the Brain

The change in circadian rhythm is not the only reason so many teens fail to get enough sleep. Social media and the electronic devices that go along with it—smartphones, tablets, computers, and video games—also lead to sleep loss. Four out of five teens have at least one of these devices in their bedrooms. It's not just the noise and the distraction that can lead to insomnia, it's the light—the blue light.

SLEEP AND THE MICROBIOME

The microbiome, or the gut microbiome, is a collection of trillions of bacteria, viruses, fungi, and protozoa (one-celled organisms such as amoebas) that live within the human stomach and intestines. While these microorganisms also live throughout the body, scientists have learned that those in the gut are especially important to our health. Humans have up to 4.4 pounds (2 kg) of these microorganisms within the gut. They help regulate hormone production and immune system function.

Much of the time, the microbiome is busy digesting the pizza you had for lunch. But the microbiome does much more than help digestion. It also releases melatonin, GABA, and other hormones that regulate sleep and emotional health. The gut microbiome has its own circadian rhythm, and the brain and microbiome are in constant communication. A disruption of either circadian rhythm affects both the microbiome and the brain and can lead to insomnia. Factors such as poor diet, stress, illness, and overuse of antibiotics can adversely affect the microbiome.

You can improve your own microbiome. Start by eating a wide variety of healthy foods, especially vegetables, beans, whole grains, and fruit. Add some fermented foods, such as yogurt, kimchi, or sauerkraut, to your regular diet. Avoid eating too much sugar and artificial sweeteners. Exercise, work to manage stress, and get enough sleep.

Thirteen-year-old Nikoli Rieger of California may not know what blue light is, but he recognizes how it affects sleep. "I think games keep kids from falling asleep. Too many screens in one day hurt your eyes and make you have pent-up energy. Kids should go to sleep at 9:00 p.m." Instead of screens at bedtime, Nikoli talks to his dog, Buddy, and his pet snake, a ball python named Void, before he goes to sleep.

Much of the light these screens emit is blue. You may not see it, but blue light is part of any bright white light such as the light coming from electronic devices. Blue light delays the release of melatonin, meaning you may find it more difficult to fall asleep when you want to. According to the National Sleep Foundation, if you read on a tablet rather than from a printed book in the evening, it may take you longer to fall asleep, and you may have less REM sleep and fewer dreams. Sleep specialist Dr. Matthew Walker says, "Compared to reading a printed book, reading on an iPad suppressed melatonin release by over 50 percent." Remember, the earlier you put your devices to bed for the night, the better your sleep will be.

Electromagnetic Spectrum

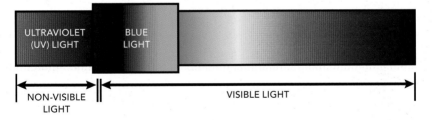

The light humans can see is part of the electromagnetic spectrum—wavelike radiation, or energy that spreads as it moves. This type of energy includes (from the longest, weakest waves to the shortest, most powerful waves): radio, microwaves, infrared, visible light, ultraviolet (UV) energy from the sun, X-rays, and gamma rays. This graph shows part of that spectrum from visible light on the right to UV light on the left. Blue light suppresses melatonin significantly and can negatively impact sleep.

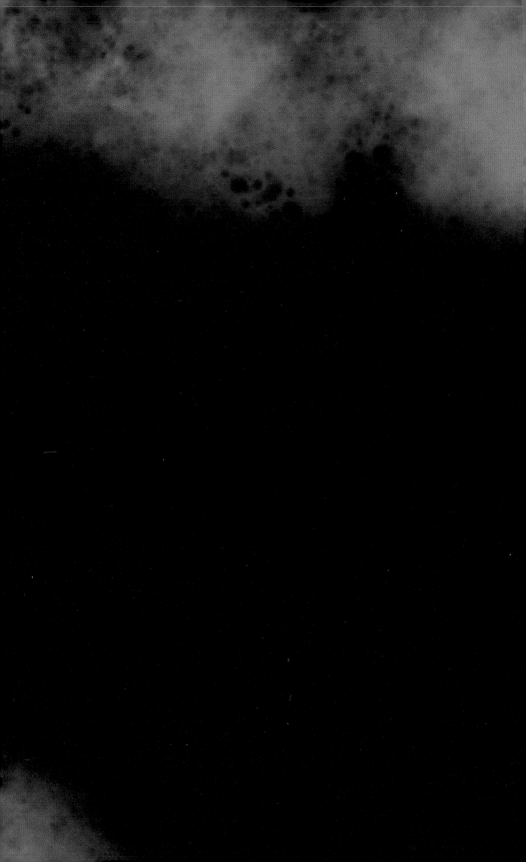

CHAPTER 4

Insomnia

Skipping sleep can be harmful—even deadly, particularly if you are behind the wheel. You can look bad, you may feel moody, and you perform poorly. Sleepiness can make it hard to get along with your family and friends and hurt your scores on school exams, on the court or on the field. A brain that is hungry for sleep will get it, even when you don't expect it.

—National Sleep Foundation, 2020

Sleep is so important to every part of the mind and body, and it feels so good that most of us want to get enough. But sometimes sleep is elusive. And all too often, teens don't get as much as they need. Every night, millions of teens face insomnia, the world's most common sleep disorder. A healthy diet, adequate exercise, and sufficient sleep make up the triad of good health.

Insomnia is

- taking a long time to fall asleep,
- waking during the night and being unable to go back to sleep, and/or
- waking too early in the morning.

While sleep is critically important during the teen years, about 87 percent of American high school teens are chronically sleep deprived. About 20 percent of teens get by on fewer than five hours of sleep per night, far from the recommended eight to ten. Juniors and seniors get even less sleep than ninth and tenth graders. Adolescence is a time of important changes—physical, intellectual, and social. Chronic insomnia can negatively impact these vital transformations and lead to or worsen serious emotional difficulties.

Insomnia has also been linked to attention deficit hyperactivity disorder (ADHD), a condition that affects brain activity. According to the American Psychiatric Association, an estimated 8.4 percent of young people aged seventeen and under have ADHD. Symptoms of ADHD include inattentiveness, hyperactivity, mood swings, poor impulse control, and trouble falling and staying asleep. Current literature suggests that some kids may be misdiagnosed with ADHD, when their symptoms may instead be related to insomnia. David Anderson, senior director of national programs and outreach at the Child Mind Institute in New York, says, "Not getting enough sleep can cause or worsen ADHD symptoms."

David DiSalvo, writing for *Forbes*, agrees. "Recent research is pointing to possible reinterpretation of ADHD as a sleep-related disorder," he says. All the more reason to be sure you get enough sleep!

Teens and Sleep

Sometimes when you can't get to sleep, it can feel as if you've got a hamster wheel spinning in endless circles inside your brain. Teens with insomnia may experience fatigue, headaches, depression, hopelessness, and anxiety. Inadequate sleep also leads to poor performance in school because of difficulties with memory, concentration, and problem-solving. Insomnia often leads to lower test scores among tired teens. Fatigue can damage relationships with friends and family. Poor sleep habits are linked to a dramatic rise in obesity and type 2 diabetes in the United States. It has been linked to acne as well. Getting enough sleep promotes both mental and physical health, which leads to improved athletic and school performance in teens.

It can be difficult to keep a healthy sleep schedule at college, according to eighteen-year-old Jack Ferris, who shares a dorm room at Washington University in Saint Louis, Missouri. "Being at college has definitely changed my sleep pattern. My classes start at 10:00 a.m. most days, so my sleep schedule is to go to bed around 1:00 a.m. even if I have to get up earlier for soccer practice," he says. "Also sharing the room with a roommate changes a lot. He has earlier classes than I do, so I wake up to his alarm. That means I often don't get enough sleep."

Not getting enough sleep affects Ferris in several ways. "I feel a general fatigue and inability to focus in class if I don't get enough sleep for one night. But after a few nights of not enough sleep, I start waking up with a sore throat," he says. "Soon enough I've got a cold that lasts a few days. Once it's gone, I feel like I'm always fighting something off. I try to stay ahead of my sleep schedule so I don't get sick again. Everyone would be a better version of themselves if they got more sleep."

Teens agree about what keeps them from getting enough sleep. The Delaney siblings—sixteen-year-old Lili and eighteen-year-old twins John and Carter—all say they don't get enough sleep. John says, "I don't get as much sleep as I want or need. I get around seven hours on school nights on a good day, but sometimes only six hours. Teens should get more sleep because if they don't, then it's not healthy for their bodies."

Carter agrees. "You can't catch up on sleep when you don't get enough. Even after just one night of not enough sleep, you are far behind. Knowing that helps me get more sleep."

All three say homework and studying keep them up late, as well as their devices. But each has a different method of falling asleep. Lili says, "I like to fall asleep watching YouTube videos."

Carter says, "I like to eat before bedtime, then brush my teeth, and apply my skin medication."

John's bedtime habits are more likely to lead to better sleep than watching videos and eating before bedtime. He says he doesn't have a particular bedtime ritual as his sister and brother have. "I usually just lie in my bed and fall asleep. Sometimes I fall asleep by accident without doing any of my nightly things like brushing my teeth and washing my face." And the twins usually sleep in different rooms. "Carter is noisy," John says, "so I sleep better in my own room."

Experts agree with Carter that you can't catch up on sleep. Dr. Cathy Goldstein, an associate professor of neurology at the University of Michigan Sleep Disorders Center in Ann Arbor, says, "You might be getting some alertness benefits by sleeping longer on the weekends, but as far as truly making up for the lost sleep during the week, you really can't make up for it hour by hour."

People may think of sleep like a bank account: withdraw an hour on a weekday, then deposit an extra hour on the weekend, and you're even. But it doesn't work that way. The National Sleep Foundation says, "Even an hour or two of lost sleep every night quickly adds up over the course of a week. Unfortunately, sleeping in for an hour or two on Saturday and Sunday mornings doesn't

HOW TIRED ARE YOU?

This questionnaire can help you figure out if you're getting enough sleep every day. Make a copy of this page or use a separate sheet of paper. Using the scale from 0–3, rank how likely you are to fall asleep in the situations below.

0 = no chance of dozing
1 = slight chance of dozing
2 = moderate chance of dozing
3 = high chance of dozing

SITUATION	CHANCE OF DOZING
Sitting and reading	_____
Watching TV	_____
Sitting in a public place such as a theater or in class	_____
As a passenger in a car for an hour without a break	_____
Lying down to rest in the afternoon	_____
Sitting and talking to a friend	_____
Sitting quietly after lunch	_____
In a car while stopped for traffic	_____

Add up the numbers to get your result.

1–6	It looks as if you're getting enough sleep.
7–8	Your score is average.
9 and up	Talk to your parents about how sleepy you feel.

really make up for all that lost time, even if you feel better on Monday in the am. All of that sleep deprivation leads to something called 'sleep debt'—the difference between the amount of sleep that you need and the amount that you're actually getting."

Getting a Later Start

To accommodate the teen circadian rhythm, some schools in the United States are moving to a later start time. The American Academy of Pediatrics recommends an 8:30 a.m. start time for high school students. However, only about 17.5 percent of American high schools meet this guideline. Some start as early as 8:00 a.m. One study showed that pushing school start times ahead by only thirty minutes increased the average sleep time for teens by forty-five minutes and allowed more than half of the students to sleep the eight hours-plus per night they need.

In 2019 California's governor signed a law moving start time to 8:30 a.m. for high school students and to 8:00 a.m. for middle grade students. Prior to that time, the average start time in the state was about 8:00 a.m., although some schools started earlier. Libby Vastano, a senior in Los Altos, California, thinks this was a good idea. "I don't know many kids that do sleep enough at my high school," she says. "If you meet someone who gets nine hours, it's like, 'Wow.'"

Wendy M. Troxel works with the RAND Corporation, a well-respected organization with a mission of improving policy and decision-making in many areas with nonpartisan research and analysis. She described an incident about teen sleep deprivation. "At 8:20 am, February 28, 2018, more than 2,500 people lost power in and around Salt Lake City [Utah] when a 17-year-old driver fell asleep at the wheel, crossed several lanes of traffic, and crashed into a power pole and power box. Miraculously . . . no one was hurt, but it could easily have been a much greater tragedy." Troxel notes that later school start times in one Utah school district led to a 70 percent reduction in auto accidents involving teens.

Driving While Drowsy

Driving while drowsy is nearly as dangerous as driving while drunk. For example, driving after going more than twenty hours

Driving while drowsy is extremely dangerous and can lead to traffic fatalities. If you are too tired to drive, ask someone else to drive or delay your trip until you are safely awake.

without sleep is the equivalent of driving with a blood-alcohol concentration of 0.08 percent, which is the legal limit for adults in the United States. (The legal limit in some states may be as low as 0.01 percent for drivers under the age of twenty-one.)

Eleventh grader Talia Dunietz knows what it's like to be tired. "As a new driver, I am aware of the risks of drunk driving, but drowsy driving was never on my radar," she says. "I am familiar with sleep deprivation and the constant need to balance schoolwork, extracurricular and social activities. On school days I leave the house at 7:20 am (often sleep deprived) and drive a short distance to school." Many teens are seriously sleep-deprived and like Talia, may not recognize it as a dangerous risk factor for accidents. "Efforts to raise awareness of drowsy driving should start now," Talia suggests.

Some driving-drowsy accidents result in tragedy. Twenty-year-old Courtney Quinn was a full-time nursing student in Pennsylvania. She also worked at a clothing store. After sleeping only three hours in a thirty-six-hour stretch, Quinn fell asleep while driving on a freeway at 70 miles (113 km) an hour. Her car drifted across several lanes of traffic and hit another car head-on going in the opposite direction. Quinn survived, but the grandmother driving the car she hit died a few hours later. The grandmother's eleven-year-old granddaughter in the back seat suffered several broken bones. Quinn was charged with involuntary manslaughter. At her sentencing, the judge told Quinn, "Your error of judgment here turned deadly. You knew you shouldn't have been behind the wheel of a car." Quinn pleaded guilty to involuntary manslaughter, and the judge sentenced her to one to two years of prison time followed by two years of probation.

Some warning signs that you are too tired to drive include these:

- yawning,
- difficulty keeping your eyes open and your head up,
- not remembering the last few miles you've driven,
- drifting out of your lane and hitting the rumble strips.

If any of these happen, or if your car alerts you that your attention is flagging, you should pull over in a safe area to take a break. Get out of the car and do some jumping jacks. Switch drivers if you're with someone. If you're alone, think about pulling over and calling a friend or your parents for a ride. It's better to be a few minutes late to your destination than to continue to drive in an unsafe condition. You wouldn't drive drunk. Now you know you shouldn't drive drowsy either.

The Caffeine Conundrum

Do you like a frothy cappuccino or a soy latte in the morning to help you wake up? Or a cup of hot tea with lemon? You're not alone. After all, 85 percent of Americans consume caffeine products every day. Caffeine can improve your reaction time, mood, and mental performance. It's even been shown to reduce the risk of heart disease. Caffeine affects you very quickly, reaching a peak level in your blood in an hour or less. Caffeine has a half-life of three to five hours.

BY THE NUMBERS

Driving while drowsy is a serious problem in the United States. Here are some statistics:

- An average of one hundred thousand drowsy-driving crashes occur each year in the United States.

- Teen drivers and young adults under the age of twenty-five cause about half of all drowsy-driving crashes.

- Four out of ten drivers admit to having fallen asleep while driving at some point in their lives.

- More than one-fourth of drivers say that during the past month, they drove while they were so tired they could barely keep their eyes open.

- If you're tired, you're three times more likely to be in a car crash.

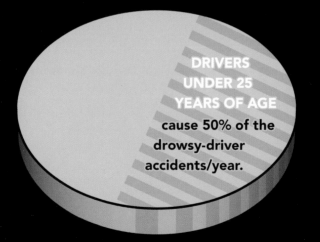

DRIVERS UNDER 25 YEARS OF AGE cause 50% of the drowsy-driver accidents/year.

Teen drivers and young adults under the age of twenty-five cause about half of all drowsy-driving crashes.

So it takes up to five hours for your body to clear half the caffeine out of your system. That can be a good thing if you're headed to school or work. But the other half of the caffeine stays in your body for several more hours, so look at the clock before you think about a second cup. Avoid all caffeine-containing products after 2:00 p.m., or you may be awake far later than you want to be in the evening.

The amount of caffeine in coffee or tea depends on how it's brewed and how much you drink. For example, an 8-ounce (237 ml) serving of coffee has about 100 mg of caffeine. An energy drink will say on the label how much caffeine it contains (usually a lot). Chocolate, colas, and even some over-the-counter medications such as cold remedies also contain caffeine. According to the University of Michigan health blogs, teens should limit their caffeine intake to one cup of coffee, one to two cups of tea, or two to three sodas per day.

> **"If you can't sleep, then get up and do something instead of lying there worrying. It's the worry that gets you, not the lack of sleep."**
>
> —*Dale Carnegie, writer and lecturer (1888–1955)*

Too much caffeine can lead to anxiety and headaches, the jitters, and insomnia. So if it's getting late and you have some homework to finish, drinking a caffeinated beverage to stay awake will likely leave you feeling crummy in the morning—not to mention that your homework may suffer. Think about reducing the amount of caffeine you drink every day, with a goal of one caffeinated drink per day.

SLEEP QUIZ

Try taking this quick quiz to see how much you have learned about healthy sleep. You can find the answers on page 92.

True or false?

1. More than one-fourth of teens say they've fallen asleep at school.

2. Seven hours of sleep at night is enough for teens.

3. If it's getting late and you still have homework, drinking a small caffeinated energy drink helps.

4. If you don't get enough sleep during the week, you can catch up on the weekend.

5. If you can't fall asleep, watching some YouTube videos will help you.

6. Getting good grades is important, so you should study well into the night before a big test.

7. Hitting the snooze button on your alarm clock lets you get a few more minutes of good sleep.

8. Getting enough sleep can improve your athletic performance.

Tricks to Fall Asleep

Psychologist and sleep specialist Dr. Michael J. Breus, clinical psychologist and fellow of the American Academy of Sleep Medicine, says that caffeine too late in the day is only one of the many things that can keep us awake at night. Other sleep inhibitors include:

- being in a room that's too warm at night;
- worrying about a school assignment or an argument with a friend;

- eating a lot before bedtime;
- anxiety and depression;
- exercising right before bedtime;
- a daytime nap longer than twenty minutes or so, since longer naps can interfere with your sleep at bedtime;
- drinking alcohol; and
- using electric devices at bedtime.

If you can't fall asleep at night, you may be tempted to get up and turn on your tablet or text your BFF. Don't. Instead of relaxing you, those activities are likely to make it even more difficult to fall asleep. Sleep experts say if you can't fall back to sleep, get out of bed and do something soothing like reading or meditating or drinking a cup of something warm and without caffeine, like milk or herbal tea. It won't be long before you're ready to climb back into bed.

But what if you've got a big test in the morning? Staying up late to study is unlikely to help you get a better grade. Experts say it's better to study in the late afternoon or early evening. And forget the snooze button on your alarm clock or smartphone. Those few minutes of extra sleep are of little help. Set your device for the actual time you need to get up, and then get up.

CHAPTER 5

Scared

> I woke up . . . feeling cold. As I went to pull the blankets
> up . . . I realized I couldn't move. I began to panic. My head
> was cemented to the pillow, my body embedded, frozen.
> Then the pressure came, pushing against my chest. Like
> something out of a bad horror movie, I tried to scream, but
> no words came out.
>
> —*Jennifer Hassan, 2018*

Jennifer Hassan, a social media editor for the *Washington Post* office based in London, knows what it's like to be terrified by a parasomnia—an abnormal event related to sleep. Some parasomnias such as sleep paralysis, nightmares, and night terrors are frightening. Other parasomnias can be downright dangerous. For example, bride-to-be Jenna Evans may have experienced a REM sleep behavior disorder that led her to swallow her engagement ring. A non-REM parasomnia led to the death of Susan Wood's son, Dalton.

Sleep Paralysis

Sleep paralysis is the temporary inability to move even though the mind and senses are fully awake. Researchers believe sleep paralysis is caused by a disturbed REM cycle because it most often happens as people fall into or come out of REM sleep. Being temporarily unable to move while dreaming is normal. It prevents people from hurting themselves by acting out a dream. But being awake and unable to move can be very frightening. People may feel as if they can't breathe, even though they are breathing.

Dr. Dan Denis at the Center for Sleep and Cognition at Beth Israel Deaconess Medical Center in Boston, Massachusetts, says, "The first time you . . . hear about [sleep paralysis], it doesn't really sound like a real thing. It sounds like something crazy, like horror movie kind of [scary]." Denis says sleep paralysis is most common in people with anxiety-specific conditions such as stress, trauma, and sometimes substance abuse. People often don't tell anyone about their sleep paralysis experiences. "And when they do talk about it, a lot of doctors and medical professionals haven't heard of it or aren't sure what it is," Denis says.

A researcher at Pennsylvania State University examined a large number of studies published over the past fifty years and found that about 20 percent of the general population have experienced sleep paralysis at least once during their lifetime. About 28 percent of students had similar experiences. The event typically lasts fewer than two minutes. The person either regains movement and gets up or falls back to sleep. Sleep paralysis often appears first in the teen years and occurs most often during a person's twenties and thirties. Stress and sleep deprivation can cause sleep paralysis, explaining why it is more common in teens and young adults, especially students.

Wendy Wright's episodes of sleep paralysis happened when she was eighteen. "I was away at college and really stressed. I missed my family. I was very shy at the time, and it took me forever to make new friends," she says. "And of course I worried about grades. I was running late one morning, so when I woke up, I tried to jump out of bed and get ready for class. But I couldn't move! My mind was working perfectly, but my body was paralyzed. I was scared and didn't understand what was happening. I just hoped a fire wouldn't break out in my dorm room! The paralysis lasted maybe two minutes and then I gasped and sat up. This happened three times during my first months of college. As time went on, I became less anxious and more comfortable with school and made new friends. It never happened again."

Dr. Clete Kushida, sleep specialist at Stanford University Center for Sleep Sciences and Medicine in California, says that people who experience sleep paralysis can try these steps to deal with the condition:

Skip the daytime nap. "Nappers seem more prone to sleep paralysis than non-nappers."

- Get as much sleep at night as possible. "There seems to be some evidence that people who are sleep deprived enter REM very quickly, which means they're still awake as their body gets paralyzed."

- Don't sleep on your back. "Sleep experts have found a correlation between sleeping in a supine position and being vulnerable to sleep paralysis."

- Seek medical care. "Because sleep paralysis might be linked to other sleep disorders . . . it's important to see a sleep specialist if your paralysis occurs often. And if you're dealing with high levels of stress or anxiety, consult a mental health professional."

Nightmares

Did you ever dream about being naked at school? Did you ever dream that you'd forgotten to study for a final exam? Did the brakes in your car fail, and you're about to plunge off a cliff? Or someone with a knife is chasing you? Sometimes you just have a bad dream. Other times, it's a true nightmare—a disturbing dream filled with terrifying images. The nightmare may wake you up because it's so frightening. Nightmares occur in REM sleep, most often later at night and into the early morning. And you'll probably remember the nightmare. In fact, you may tell your friends about your nightmare the next day because it's likely to be a vivid memory.

Nightmares are twice as common among girls as boys. Among sixteen-year-olds, about 20 percent of boys have nightmares, while 40 percent of girls do. Scientists found that teens who experience frequent nightmares may be at increased risk for suicide attempts or self-harm, although the exact reason why is not known.

According to *Psychology Today*, the causes of nightmares include anxiety and stress, trauma, the death of a loved one, chronic sleep deprivation, jet lag, illness and fever, reading scary books or seeing scary movies before sleep, and side effects of medications, drugs, and alcohol. Nightmares are more common in families with a history of nightmares or other parasomnias, such as talking or walking during sleep.

The authors of a study published in the *Journal of Clinical Psychiatry* said, "Further research needs to examine the mediators and moderators and biological mechanisms of the nightmare-self harm link and the effects of intervention programs that target coping with distress associated with frequent nightmares in adolescents." The study said the findings were so important that physicians should ask teens during routine physical exams how often they have nightmares.

THE NIGHTMARE

Sleep paralysis is so universal that about one hundred words worldwide in different languages are used to describe it. People interpret events that they cannot understand—such as sleep paralysis—in the context of their culture. The eighteenth-century painting *The Nightmare*, by the Swiss English artist Henry Fuseli, shows an incubus, an evil spirit, squatting on a sleeping woman who is likely experiencing sleep paralysis.

Henry Fuseli created this oil painting—*The Nightmare*—of a sleeping woman with an apelike incubus sitting on her chest. The word "nightmare" comes from *night* plus *maere*, an Old English word for "incubus." The artwork was first exhibited in London in 1782 and was an instant success.

At that time, people feared the incubus would come to them at night to suffocate or rape them. Other cultures believed a demon or vampire would choke them or suck their breath.

A person in modern times may interpret sleep paralysis as being abducted by aliens and taken to a UFO for experiments. One study found that nearly four million Americans believe they've been abducted by aliens. Kazuhiko Fukuda, a psychologist at Edogawa University in Japan and a leading expert on sleep paralysis, said in a *New York Times* article, "If Americans have the experience [of sleep paralysis] and if they have heard of alien abductions, then they may think, 'Aha, it's alien abduction!'"

Night Terrors

Night terrors are not nightmares. They usually occur during the first half of the night while the sleeper is in stage 3 of non-REM sleep. During these frightening episodes, people may scream out loud. They will have dilated pupils and fearful eyes. They may sit up and even sleepwalk. The heart rate increases, breathing speeds up, and the person may be drenched in sweat. An episode usually lasts a few minutes, although some last much longer. Journalist Darlena Cunha wrote in the *Washington Post* about her six-year-old daughter's night terrors.

> The piercing scream wakes me up from a dead sleep. As I stumble down the hallway, bumping into walls to get to my child as quickly as possible, I hear the next phase already beginning. 'No. Leave me alone. Stop. STOP,' [the child screams]. My baby is petrified. And she's all alone. . . . Even though I'm in the room now, lifting her up, sitting her on my lap, she can't see me. She can't feel me. She is lost, eyes open wide, seeing things that aren't there. Awake in her sleep, but not present. She's having another night terror. . . . But I can't [leave her alone, although doctors advise parents to do just that]. I can't watch her sit up stark straight and shout in abject horror against foes she cannot escape.

> **"My sleep wasn't peaceful, though. I have the sense of emerging from a world of dark, haunted places where I traveled alone."**
>
> —*Suzanne Collins, author of The Hunger Games trilogy (1962–)*

According to the Mayo Clinic, night terrors, sometimes called sleep terrors, affect up to 40 percent of children between the ages of four and twelve, although they can occur at any age. Most people outgrow night terrors by their teen years. Stress, fatigue, travel, and fever increase the chance of night terrors. Children having night terrors are asleep and very difficult to rouse. If someone does wake them up, they're confused and have little or no memory of the terrifying episode. Occasional sleep terrors aren't generally a cause for concern, according to the National Sleep Foundation. However, if the episodes become frequent, disrupt the sleep of other family members, or pose the potential for accidental injury or harm, it's a good idea to consult a sleep specialist.

DO SCARY MOVIES GIVE YOU NIGHTMARES?

Can movies frighten you into nightmares? Maybe yes. Maybe no. Even experts aren't quite sure what impact scary movies have on your sleep. An article in the *Huffington Post* said, "Turns out Mom was being a little paranoid when she warned against watching horror flicks before bedtime."

Nemours, a national nonprofit organization based in Jacksonville, Florida, that promotes child and teen health, leaves the door open. "Sometimes nightmares are part of a child's reaction to trauma—such as a natural disaster, accident, or injury. For some kids, especially those with a good imagination, reading scary books or watching scary movies or TV shows just before bedtime can inspire nightmares." Nightmares may contain recognizable bits of the day's events with a frightening twist.

Dr. Gary Levinson, sleep expert at San Diego's Sharp Memorial Hospital, says, "Nightmares can be caused by any stress that leads to anxiety. . . . Given the intense multisensory stimulus one gets from horror movies, especially when watched at night prior to bedtime, the brain could perceive this as a form of virtual reality, evoking typical stressful situations of real life." Bottom line? If scary movies at night make their way into your dreams and give you nightmares, watch them in the daytime instead.

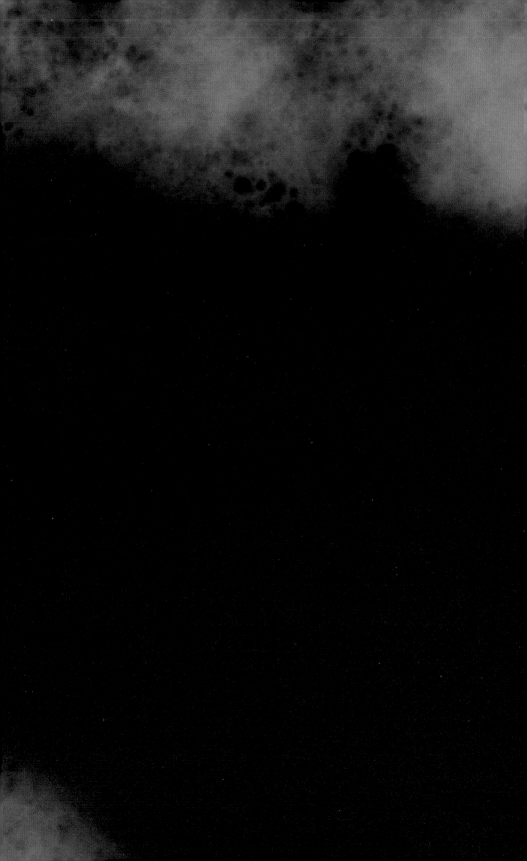

CHAPTER 6

Sleepwalking

I fall asleep and I have a dream that there is a guided missile headed towards my room, and there are all these military personnel in the room, and I jump out of bed, and I say: What's the plan? And they say the missile coordinates are set specifically on you. And I decided in my dream and, as it turns out, in my life, to jump out my window.

—*Mike Birbiglia, 2010*

Comedian Mike Birbiglia wrote the book *Sleepwalk with Me* about his sleepwalking experiences. During an interview with National Public Radio, he described an episode that occurred while he was sleeping at a hotel. "So I jumped through the window, fell two stories, landed on the front lawn of the hotel, got up and kept running." Birbiglia ended up in an emergency room with broken glass in his legs. He needed more than thirty stitches to repair the damage.

A sleep doctor diagnosed Birbiglia with REM sleep behavior disorder in which the paralysis that normally occurs during REM sleep is absent. Without the paralysis, people may act out their dreams as Birbiglia did. "People who have this [disorder] are commonly running away from some kind of demon or wild animal," Birbiglia said.

Walking While Sleeping

Sleepwalking is a parasomnia, an abnormal behavior associated with sleep. Sleepwalking can occur during the stages of deep sleep as well as while dreaming during REM sleep. Although the causes are different, both types of sleepwalking have the potential to cause injury to the sleeping person or others. Sleep expert Wytrzes explains it this way:

> Non-REM sleepwalking, which includes childhood sleepwalking and sleep talking, occurs during a partial arousal from deep sleep that happens while the brain is still maturing. The sleeping brain doesn't quite have its act together as it cycles from one stage to the next so the brain is half awake and half asleep. Young sleepers can usually maneuver around obstacles such as a chair or table in their surroundings. Most children outgrow these episodes as the brain matures. Rarely does this type of sleepwalking persist into young adulthood. The episodes seldom result in injury and most non-REM sleepwalkers transition back to sleep without fully awakening.

Rarely, non-REM sleepwalking episodes may cause injury or even death. Susan Wood's son Dalton died during a non-REM episode of sleepwalking early in the morning. Dalton was not awake enough to know what he was doing. Some people with non-REM sleepwalking have gotten into their cars and driven long distances without being aware of it. Non-REM sleepwalkers are unlikely to remember their episodes of sleepwalking.

Birbiglia's REM sleep behavior disorder is very different from non-REM parasomnia. According to Wytrzes, "[REM sleep behavior disorder] occurs because REM sleep becomes abnormal, often due to a neurological disorder that interferes with normal brain chemistry. During REM, our brains are active, but our bodies are paralyzed," she says. "With REM sleep behavior disorder, patients lose the normal paralysis of REM sleep and can literally act out their dreams. It's more common with adults, and injuries are more common because the sleepwalker is older and the dreams may be threatening or scary. Patients may punch, kick, and try to run away, making them prone to accidents." Sometimes REM sleep behavior disorder may be associated with neurological problems such as early onset of Parkinson's disease.

Birbiglia jumped through a glass window to escape the missile headed toward him, while Jenna Evans swallowed her engagement ring to keep it safe from robbers. Birbiglia and Evans both experienced these episodes of REM sleep behavior disorder as they were soundly asleep and dreaming. People who experience REM sleep behavior disorder will usually remember the nightmares that caused their episodes.

Who Sleepwalks and When?

About 3.6 percent of American adults are sleepwalkers, while up to 40 percent of children and teens sleepwalk. Sleepwalking is most likely to occur when sleep deprived, when stressed or anxious, with fevers, and when using alcohol or certain medications.

Susan Wood attributes her son Dalton's death in part to sleep deprivation. "While Dalton had no previous history of sleepwalking that I knew of, he snored and frequently talked in his sleep," she says. "Add physical fatigue to this already disturbed sleep—he'd

Sleepwalking is a popular subject of paintings, operas, novels, plays, and movies. This 1871 painting by English artist John Everett Millais is called *The Somnambulist*, another word for sleepwalker. Although this painting depicts an adult woman, the sleeping disorder is much more common in children and teens than adults.

worked five consecutive days at his new job, three of those after a full school day that started at 6 a.m. This put him at even greater risk for a non-REM parasomnia. When I'd picked Dalton up after work that Sunday afternoon, he told me how tired he was. We'd agreed it was a good thing the next day was Memorial Day so he'd be able to sleep in."

Some of the very medications prescribed for insomnia, such as sleeping pills and sedatives, can worsen sleepwalking behaviors. Dr. Jesse Mindel, a sleep medicine specialist with the Ohio State University Wexner Medical Center in Columbus, Ohio, says, "These meds appear to bind to receptors in the brain that may allow someone to move around more than usual while staying asleep."

Stress can also trigger sleepwalking. "My son Ethan began sleepwalking when he started a new high school," Carol Ridenour says. "That was a particularly stressful time for him. He carried sandwiches and ice cream to his bedroom, but never ate the food. It seemed like I was always wiping up melted ice cream.

One night, he apparently thought he was in the bathroom. He lifted a cushion from a living room chair, urinated into the chair, and lowered the cushion as if he was at the toilet." Ridenour was especially concerned early one morning when she found the front door unlocked and Ethan standing on the porch totally asleep wearing only his pajama bottoms. "I got worried he might hurt himself. I installed locks on all the doors—locks he couldn't open in his sleep. Fortunately, the sleepwalking episodes lasted only a few months."

Like night terrors, sleepwalking tends to run in families as Susan Wood learned a few months after her son's death. "Last fall my daughter had to start waking up at 5:45 a.m. instead of 6:45 a.m. to catch the bus to her new high school. She was tired all the time and had two episodes of sleepwalking that I know of," Wood said.

SLEEP DRIVING

Some people walk in their sleep. A few others talk in their sleep. And rarely, someone drives in their sleep. Sleep specialist Dr. W. Chris Winter tells of one incident in his book *The Sleep Solution*. One of his first cases of sleep driving was a college student who left her dorm wearing nothing but tiny shorts and a tank top. She got into her car and took off. She drove for a while until she got confused. She pulled over and called her parents, five hours away, and said, "'Dad, can you come get me?' He answered, 'Sweetheart, it will take me hours to get to you. What's going on? It's 3:00 in the morning. . . . Where are you?' She said, 'Oh, just forget it,'" and hung up.

Fortunately, the police soon found the girl and got her back to her dorm safely. The next morning, she couldn't remember anything about what had happened the night before or the call to her parents. While sleep driving has happened to people taking sleeping pills, it occasionally happens to people like this college student for no apparent reason.

"Like Dalton, she'd never been a sleepwalker before. Thankfully, she didn't leave the house or harm herself in any way. But it shocked me enough to purchase an alarm for the front door, which I activate every night as we go to bed. It was easy to install and gives me peace of mind."

Talking While Sleeping

Did your best friend ever rat you out? While she was asleep? Madison often talked in her sleep. Madison's mom would sometimes sit her up in bed and ask her questions. Although Madison was still partially asleep, she carried on conversations with her mom and never remembered what happened the next day.

Sleep talking can occur during any stage of sleep. Speech is most understandable in stages 1 and 2 when people, such as Madison, can have entire conversations with other people that make perfect sense. In stage 3 (deep sleep) and REM sleep, sleep talking often consists of gibberish and sounds rather than words. Stress, depression, fatigue, alcohol, and fever can trigger sleep talking. It often occurs with other sleep disorders such as nightmares, sleepwalking, and REM sleep behavior disorder.

Madison and Chloe were best friends, and Chloe should have been at the big high school graduation party at Madison's house. But Chloe didn't show up, and Madison's mom noticed. When Madison's mom woke her halfway up and asked where Chloe was, Madison said she'd spent the night with her boyfriend. Madison's mom told Chloe's mom, and she grounded Chloe for two months.

The medical profession has no particular treatment for sleep talking. But getting enough sleep and following a regular sleep schedule may reduce the frequency. However, if sleep talking persists over a long time, see a doctor to be sure there is no underlying medical problem such as severe stress or anxiety or an undiagnosed sleep disorder.

CHAPTER 7

Sleep Apnea

Sleep apnea is literally when a person stops breathing during sleep. As a result, the brain undergoes repeated moments of suffocating. In popular culture, snoring is viewed as funny. . . . The reality is this loud snort is often the person gasping for air, as the brain is not getting enough oxygen.

—Dr. Paul G. Mathew, assistant professor of neurology at Harvard Medical School, Cambridge, Massachusetts, 2017

Do your siblings, parents, or friends say that you sometimes stop breathing when you sleep and then snort and gasp for air when you start breathing again? And do you find you're tired and irritable during the day even if it seems you got enough sleep? If so, it's possible you have sleep apnea—a potentially serious condition in which people stop and start breathing throughout the night.

When people stop breathing—even for a few seconds—their bodies don't get enough oxygen. Some people may stop breathing one hundred or more times a night. While sleep apnea is more common in older people, it happens to children and teens as well.

What Causes Sleep Apnea?

An estimated ninety million Americans snore, and about twenty-two million of them are likely to have sleep apnea. The most common form of sleep apnea is caused by a partial blockage in the airway. This is called obstructive sleep apnea (OSA). It could be the tongue falling back into the throat. It can also be the upper palate—the roof of your mouth—relaxing and drooping into your airway when you sleep. OSA doesn't allow sufficient air to reach the lungs. Causes of OSA include these:

- Enlarged tonsils or adenoids that partially block the airway. Years ago, doctors routinely removed these organs, which are part of the body's immune system. That surgery is no longer performed as often. Many young people still have their tonsils and adenoids.
- Narrow airways. Some people with thicker necks naturally have narrower airways.
- Use of alcohol, sleeping pills, or sedatives. These can relax the muscles in the throat and tongue and may cause sleep apnea.
- Stuffy noses. People who have difficulty breathing through their noses due to allergies or other problems are more prone to sleep apnea because less air passes through their nostrils. This may lead to mouth breathing, which tends to dry out the airways.
- Excess weight. Obesity greatly increases the risk of sleep apnea. Fat deposits around the upper airway can obstruct breathing.

Excess weight is by far the most common cause of OSA. Obesity is on the rise in the United States, affecting teens and adults alike. "The obesity epidemic is not limited to adults. More teens are overweight than ever," says sleep specialist Wytrzes. Every two years, the CDC monitors the incidence of various health-related behaviors—such as smoking, drug use, and obesity—that affect American youth. The CDC's 2017 survey found that nearly 15 percent of high school students were obese while more than 15 percent were overweight according to their body mass index. About one out of three adolescents are obese or overweight.

BODY MASS INDEX

Body mass index, or BMI, is the numeric relationship between a person's weight and height. Doctors use BMI charts—not how a patient looks—to determine if their patients are in a healthy height-to-weight range. For children and teens nineteen years and younger, the healthy BMI range is different from the range for adult BMIs because young people are still growing, and a healthy weight varies by age, height, and gender.

These charts measure BMI by percentile. For example, a BMI at the 60th percentile means that out of one hundred people the same age, height, and gender, sixty people will weigh less, and forty people will weigh more. A percentile between 5 and 85 is considered a healthy BMI for a teen. Percentiles in the 85 to 94 range are overweight. Children and teens with a BMI at or above the 95th percentile are obese. The easiest way to determine a young person's BMI is to use the CDC online calculator at **https://www.cdc.gov/healthyweight/bmi/calculator.html**.

Overweight and obese teens with sleep apnea face other health risks including diabetes and heart disease. And psychological issues are just as troubling. One study showed that teens suffering from obstructive sleep apnea have more problems with attention, hyperactivity, aggressiveness, managing social situations, and difficulties controlling their emotions. Michelle Perfect, assistant professor at the University of Arizona in Tucson, says, "If left untreated, OSA negatively impacts a youth's ability to regulate their behaviors, emotions and social interactions. These behaviors can interfere with their ability to care for themselves and engage in socially appropriate behaviors—skills that are needed to be successful in school."

According to the Alaska Sleep Education Center, "OSA is a growing health problem among adolescents yet the risk factors of untreated and severe OSA among teens are not well understood. . . . Adolescents who have obstructive sleep apnea are faced nightly with the repeated stopping and starting of breathing during sleep." So if the clock says you're getting enough sleep and you still feel tired every day, talk to your doctor.

How Do Doctors Test for Sleep Apnea?

"As information about the effects of untreated sleep apnea in teens becomes more widely known, more teens are undergoing sleep testing," says Wytrzes. If a sleep medicine specialist suspects you may have sleep apnea, they will recommend a sleep study (also called a polysomnography) to study your sleep. During a sleep study, a technician at a sleep clinic places brain-monitoring electrodes on your face and scalp. These electrodes sense the electrical activity in your brain that shows when you enter and leave the different stages of sleep. The technician places other electrodes on your chest to monitor your heartbeat.

You then spend the night at the clinic. The room where you sleep is dark, quiet, and comfortable. You can bring your own pajamas, a special pillow, and even your favorite teddy bear. The doctor will tell you to sleep on your back if possible, because it's easier to detect sleep apnea in that position. As you sleep, machines measure your brain waves, heart rate, and breathing. A plastic device clipped to your finger measures oxygen levels in your blood. One of the machines is an electroencephalogram (EEG), which documents your brain waves as you pass through each stage of sleep. The results guide doctors to a better understanding of your sleep patterns. And even if you don't sleep through the entire night, the experts will gain enough information from the sleep study to figure out what's going on with you. After they evaluate the results, the professionals will offer you and your parents treatment options that might benefit you.

While specialized sleep clinics provide the best results for sleep tests, more at-home testing is being developed. For a young person with possible sleep apnea not complicated by an underlying medical condition, home-testing devices called sleep trackers are available. Some are small enough to wear on your wrist, while others may clip to your pillow or sit on your bedside

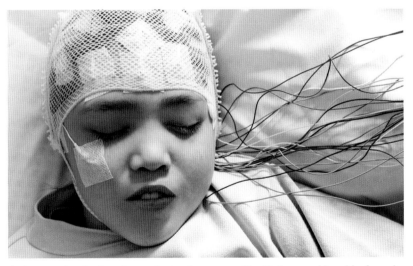

A sleep technologist places electrodes on a patient's face and head before she begins an overnight sleep study. The next morning, a physician will study the scans of the patient's brain waves to see how well that person has slept. With that information, the doctor will suggest a plan for improving sleep.

table. The tracker monitors and measures sleep duration, sleep quality (determined by how often the person tosses and turns during the night), sleep phases, and environmental factors such as temperature and light in the bedroom.

The trackers collect a lot of information about your sleep. Yet Dr. Alan Schwartz, director of the Sleep Disorders Center at Johns Hopkins Bayview Medical Center in Baltimore, Maryland, says, "They don't measure sleep directly. Most sleep tracking devices make some guesstimate as to how much you're actually sleeping." The trackers can provide graphs and reports, but Schwartz says, "Just take the numbers with a grain of salt." If the results concern you or your parents, see a sleep specialist to determine if you need testing for sleep apnea.

> **"I find the nights long, for I sleep but little, and think much."**
>
> —*Charles Dickens, British author (1812–1870)*

Can Sleep Apnea Be Managed?

If you have sleep apnea, your doctor may recommend an oral appliance to help control the condition. This device looks much like a sports mouth guard. The appliance moves your jaw and tongue forward to keep the upper airway open. Patients who would benefit from a mouth guard consult a dentist, who measures the patient's jaw and mouth and fits the appliance.

Some teens may need minor surgical procedures to manage their apnea. If the cause of your sleep apnea is enlarged tonsils, adenoids, or both, the doctor might suggest a simple outpatient procedure to remove them. Some people may need surgery on the

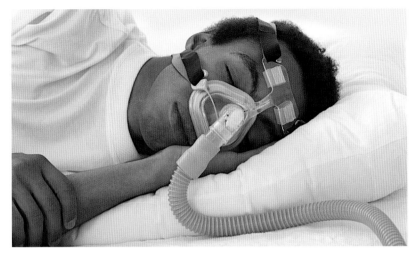

The CPAP machine is an excellent way to manage sleep apnea. The device is considered to be "durable medical equipment," so most insurance companies will cover the cost. Be sure to ask to be certain.

soft palate or the uvula (the small piece of skin that hangs above the throat) to help keep the airway open.

These methods may not help people with severe obstructive sleep apnea. For those people, the doctor may recommend a continuous positive airway pressure machine, or CPAP. This small machine lies in the bed next to the sleeper's pillow or sits on a bedside table, and people wear a mask over their nose while sleeping. The CPAP gently blows air through a tube and into the mask. The machine pressurizes the air to keep the airway open while the person sleeps. And keeping the airway open is vital, especially during REM sleep when muscle tone in the throat is less than normal.

The machine is more comfortable than it looks. And it's quiet, making about the same amount of noise as a whisper or a ticking clock. A doctor helps the patient find the right size and model of CPAP machine. For tweens and teens who are still growing, the doctor will adjust the mask every now and then. According to Wytrzes, the CPAP machine is the most effective treatment for moderate to severe sleep apnea.

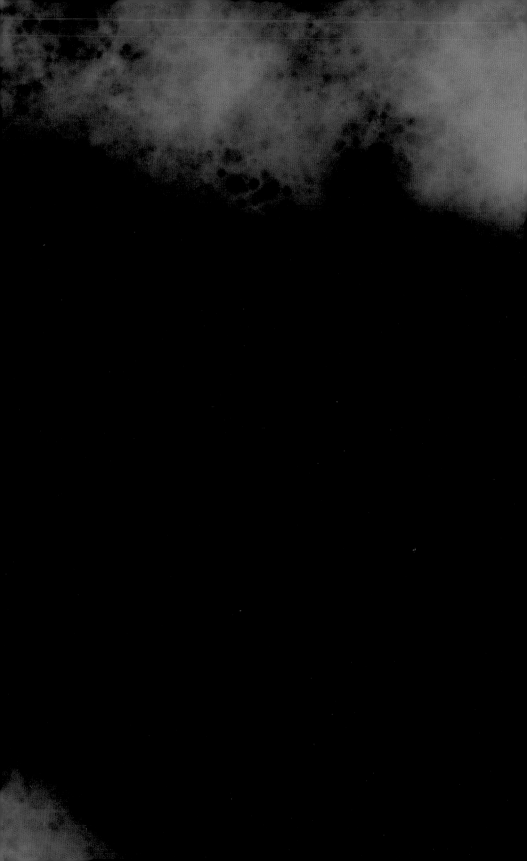

CHAPTER 8
Sleepers Seeking Help

More than a quarter of us [Americans] feel tired five to seven days a week. Some attribute their drowsiness to not getting enough sleep, while others claim poor sleep quality is to blame. Ultimately, most people drink a cup of coffee and go about their day without adjusting their bedtime routines. As a result, they repeat the same poor sleep cycle week after week.

—*National Sleep Foundation, 2020*

If you're tired week after week, month after month, and your schoolwork and social life are suffering, you may be desperate to find something to help you get more sleep. If this happens, talk to your parents or another trusted adult and your doctor. Some insomnia remedies, such as prescription sleeping pills, can be potentially harmful. Other treatments, such as cognitive behavioral therapy, a form of psychological treatment, can help with insomnia.

You're not alone in your wish for better sleep. The global market for sleep-related services and products is huge. Market researchers believe it will reach about $102 billion by 2023. Some of these products and services may work for you, while others may not. It's important to be well informed.

Prescription Sleeping Pills

Stacie C. had trouble sleeping, so her doctor prescribed Ambien, a common sleeping pill. While Stacie was on Ambien, she would take food to bed or post online. In the morning, she wouldn't remember any of it. "I didn't think it was that big of a deal, so I stayed on it [Ambien]," Stacie said in *Women's Health* magazine. "One night, toward the end of my time on Ambien, I woke up in my car. I was in my pajamas, driving and crying. I knew where I was, but I had no idea how I got there, and I didn't know why I was crying, either. I pulled into a parking lot and waited until I was done crying for no apparent reason, and then I just drove back home. It had to have been like 3 o'clock in the morning." Stacie went to see a new doctor, who immediately took her off the Ambien.

Medications that promote sleep are called hypnotics. These include sleeping pills such as those with the brand names Ambien, Lunesta, and Sonata. They also include sedatives such as the brand names Valium, Librium, and Xanax. Although about nine million Americans take prescription medications for insomnia, they should be used as a last resort rather than a first step. Sleep specialist Matthew Walker says, "No past or current sleeping medications on the legal (or illegal) market induce natural sleep." Walker points out that when patients take these medications, their EEGs show their brains do not produce the waves of deepest sleep—the sleep we need the most. He also points to a number of sleep medication studies that show that sleeping pills have no more benefit than a placebo.

BLACK BOX WARNING

The Food and Drug Administration (FDA) monitors the safety of prescription medications in the United States. When evidence shows a drug can cause a potentially dangerous reaction, the FDA requires the manufacturer of that drug to put a black box warning on the label. This means that the drug is potentially fatal or disabling and that the risks may outweigh the benefits.

Since April 2019, the FDA has required black box warnings for several common prescription sleeping medications including Ambien, Sonata, and Lunesta. The FDA found that "rare but serious injuries have happened with certain common prescription insomnia medicines because of sleep behaviors, including sleepwalking, sleep driving, and engaging in other activities while not fully awake. These complex sleep behaviors have also resulted in deaths." The FDA warned that such events can occur after just one dose of the medication.

Journalist Teresa Carr, writing about a 2018 survey in *Consumer Reports*, said, "One thing all these medications have in common: limited benefits. Sleep drugs can help people fall asleep faster or return to sleep if they wake up in the middle of the night, but the benefits are usually modest."

Dr. Daniel Buysse, endowed chair in sleep medicine and professor of psychiatry and clinical and translational science at the University of Pittsburgh School of Medicine in Pittsburgh, Pennsylvania, added, "Most only increase total sleep time by about 20 to 30 minutes."

Usually the risk of side effects, such as feeling drowsy, confused, or forgetful the next day, outweighs the benefits of sleeping pills. Three percent of people admitted to dozing off while driving after taking sleeping pills the night before. Anyone thinking about prescription sleeping pills must compare the relatively high risk with the relatively low benefit.

Occasionally doctors may recommend prescription sleeping pills for a teen with severe insomnia. These should be used only for a short time because they can lead to dependency. They also may cause rebound insomnia when discontinued. You may have even more trouble sleeping after you stop taking them. Sleeping pills can also interact with other medications you may be taking, and people with certain medical conditions should not take them. Don't ever take other people's medications, especially sleeping pills or sedatives. Unexpected interactions could be dangerous.

Over-the-Counter Sleep Aids

Over-the-counter (OTC) products and supplements—those not requiring a doctor's prescription—for insomnia include a number of medications, herbs, and teas. Some of these products may be helpful, but others have the potential for harm. Many are promoted as natural, but natural is not the same as safe. Vegetables raised without pesticides are natural. So are poisonous mushrooms. One is good for your health, and the other will kill you. The FDA oversees the safety of prescription medications in the United States. But the FDA has no authority over supplements. You can find many of these items in drugstores and natural food stores. But OTC medications and supplements may not be safe. And some can interact with prescription medications. Always check with your parents and your doctor about supplements if you take any prescription medications.

Here are some common supplements that drugstores and other stores are likely to carry that promise to promote sleep:

- Melatonin. If our body produces melatonin to help us get to sleep, wouldn't it be helpful to take more of it? The Mayo Clinic says that OTC melatonin supplements may help people experiencing jet lag and may help insomnia with short-term use. It's generally safe, but may cause headaches, dizziness, and nausea. Evidence about the long-term effectiveness of melatonin supplements has not been proven.

- Valerian. This herbal supplement is made from the roots of a flowering plant. According to the Mayo Clinic, valerian may reduce the amount of time it takes you to fall asleep and may help you sleep better. Studies have not shown what dosage is safe or how long you should take it. Side effects such as headaches, dizziness, stomach problems, and insomnia may occur (worsening the problem you take it for).

- Kava. This supplement comes from a plant native to certain islands in the Pacific Ocean. It has an effect much like alcohol. It may help with insomnia, but it can have serious side effects, including depression and diarrhea. Kava has been linked to liver disease and death. Never take it without talking to a doctor first.

- Tea. Some kinds of tea may help relax you, but be sure the one you try doesn't contain caffeine. While generally safe, calming teas have few studies to confirm their effectiveness. Many people feel that chamomile tea helps them sleep better. Teas made with lavender and lemon balm may help some people. Drinking a warm, non-caffeinated beverage at bedtime may relax you enough to help you fall sleep.

- Diphenhydramine. Sold under the brand name Benadryl, this antihistamine is a medication usually taken for allergies. One of its side effects is drowsiness, so some people take it to help their sleep. Other side effects include dry mouth, blurred vision, and constipation. It may make some people very tired the next day. Talk to your parents or doctor about using any products containing diphenhydramine. Diphenhydramine is also found in OTC sleeping pills such as Aleve PM and Unisom.

GROUP THERAPY AND THE INTERNET

A randomized controlled trial is a medical study in which groups of participants are randomly assigned to receive different types of medications and interventions. For example, one group of participants in a study will receive one of several interventions without knowing which one they are taking. Another group—called the control group—receives no treatment at all. This allows researchers to determine whether the treatment for an illness or condition worked any better than no treatment.

A study to examine cognitive behavior therapy for insomnia (CBT-I) in teens took place in 2015. Researchers randomly divided 116 teens, with an average age of 15.6 years, into three groups. The first group received CBT-I in six weekly group therapy sessions under the guidance of two sleep therapists. The second group worked through a guided online self-help website, receiving written feedback from a sleep therapist. The third group—the control group—were told they were on a waiting list for CBT-I therapy and received no treatment.

The results showed that the first and second groups greatly benefited from the CBT-I whether in a group setting or online. Both groups showed clinically significant improvement in their sleep patterns as measured subjectively (the teens telling researchers how they felt) and objectively (with researchers measuring sleep times and reviewing sleep logs). Researchers concluded when possible that "we recommend CBT-I as treatment for adolescent insomnia. Internet treatment of adolescent insomnia should be promoted in mental health organizations."

A 2019 study of adults looked at CBT-I delivered by telemedicine—remote diagnosis and treatment of patients by health-care professionals via a video link. The study showed that this technique is just as effective as when delivered in person. Telemedicine may be applied to adolescents living in remote areas who are unable to attend therapy sessions in person.

One of the most common reasons people give for taking OTC drugs is because they thought the OTC medications were safer than prescription sleeping pills. "But the sedating effects of OTC drugs frequently linger into the next day," Carr said. In fact, 40 percent of respondents taking an OTC sleep drug said that they felt foggy or drowsy the next morning, compared with 32 percent of those taking a prescription drug." Antihistamines may also lead to confusion, constipation, dry mouth, and trouble urinating.

> **"A well spent day brings happy sleep."**
>
> —*Leonardo da Vinci, Italian painter (1452–1519)*

Cognitive Behavioral Therapy

Cognitive behavioral therapy (CBT) is a talk therapy in which a person works with a counselor or therapist. During the sessions, the therapist helps the person identify negative thoughts and reframe them in a more positive way. With this skill, people can better recognize and manage emotional, behavioral, and physical challenges. CBT is often used to treat depression and other mental health issues.

Therapists are increasingly using CBT to help people with insomnia. When used to treat insomnia, this therapy is called CBT-I. (The I stands for "insomnia.") CBT-I is a structured program that helps a person replace thoughts and behaviors that lead to insomnia with habits that promote sleep. Compared to sleeping pills, CBT-I is very safe, has no dangerous side effects, and the effects seem to last.

A CBT-I sleep therapist will begin the program by asking you to complete a detailed sleep diary for a week or two. You'll document when you go to bed and when you get up, how you slept, what activities occurred during the day or before bedtime, and other sleep-related information. Based on your diary, the sleep therapist will suggest one or more of the following CBT-I techniques.

- Sleep restriction. Avoid naps, set specific times for sleep and awakening, and reduce the time spent in bed. If you spend too much time awake in bed, the act of being in bed may become associated in your mind with poor sleep. Sleep restriction can lead to temporary mild sleep deprivation, which makes it easier to fall asleep at night.
- Sleep hygiene. Learn how to avoid habits that affect sleep. These include smoking, drinking alcohol, drinking caffeine late in the day, and not getting enough exercise. Learn how to wind down before bedtime. Think about a non-device activity that relaxes you, and do that in the evening before bed.
- Sleep environment. Create a comfortable place to sleep by keeping your bedroom cool, dark, and quiet. Keep television and electronic devices out of your bedroom. If you don't have window coverings, put up light-blocking shades or heavy curtains. And don't look at the clock. Some people turn their clock to face away from them.
- Biofeedback. Patients with insomnia that is linked to anxiety, muscle tension, an inability to relax, and racing thoughts are good candidates for biofeedback. Sleep therapists show patients how to use a biofeedback monitor to measure heart rate, breathing, and muscle tension. If stress levels are high, you can learn how to slow your heart rate and breathing, and how to relax your muscles. The therapist may give you a biofeedback machine to take home for a while to help improve your sleep.

CBT-I may seem challenging at first and is likely to take a few visits before you can manage the techniques your sleep therapist recommends. You may even feel more tired at first as the therapists says no to naps and advises you to stay up later than you normally do.

CBD

A new treatment for insomnia may be on the horizon. As of January 2020, thirty-three states have approved cannabis (marijuana) for medical use. It is still illegal at the federal level.

The cannabis plant contains two ingredients: tetrahydrocannabinol (THC), which alters the mental state, and cannabidiol (CBD), which does not. CBD is a legal ingredient in various products. Among other things, it is used successfully to treat some types of seizures in children. Parents using it for their children's seizures have found it also helps their children with anxiety and sleep. CBD can be added to certain kinds of edible gummy candies and liquid drops. These edibles have been shown to gradually reduce anxiety and increase relaxation to help with sleep.

Medical professionals are hopeful that CBD will help with a wide range of other conditions. However, more studies need to be done on the long-term effects of CBD in all age groups. It has the potential to interact with a number of prescription drugs. CBD products can be expensive too. Always talk to your parents or a trusted adult and consult with your doctor before trying a CBD product.

But CBT-I can help nearly everyone who has insomnia and can help you break the bad habits that may keep you from getting as much sleep as you want. Stick with it.

Christine was a swimming instructor for the US Navy. She had serious problems with insomnia. The National Sleep Foundation described her experience with CBT-I in an article on its website. Some of the therapy, such as giving up daytime naps, was difficult. Christine said, "I went with an open mind, but I didn't expect [CBT-I] to work as well as it did. Now I can go to bed and sleep on my own, which many people take for granted—but for me it is the biggest gift of all."

CHAPTER 9
Sleeping Better, Sleeping Longer

Focus your mind on something like a mental picture or story. By putting all of your attention on something specific, you can escape from the cycle of going over and over the thoughts that are running through your brain and keeping you up. You'll quickly feel more calm, positive, and peaceful.

—*National Sleep Foundation, 2019*

Can you think your way to better sleep? Sleep experts say yes. Several easy activities that you can do at home may decrease the stress and anxiety that get in the way of sleep. These emotions especially affect REM sleep, the very sleep we need the most to remain healthy. Depression can cause insomnia, and insomnia can cause depression—a cycle of unhealthy consequences.

In fact, people with insomnia are four times more likely to become depressed than people who get enough sleep.

Think about It

Meditation is the practice of relaxing your body and focusing your mind on restful and pleasant thoughts. Practiced regularly, experts say it can help promote sleep. Meditation begins with finding a comfortable spot to sit or to lie down. Next, close your eyes and breathe slowly and deeply. Visualize a place or activity that calms you down. Maybe it's a morning hike in the woods, an afternoon at the beach, or looking at the moon with a friend. Focus your mind on that.

> **"Early to bed and early to rise makes a man healthy, wealthy, and wise."**
>
> —*Benjamin Franklin (1706–1790), American Founding Father*

Meditation slows your pulse, lowers your blood pressure, and decreases stress hormones. Some people meditate in a class with other people, with a mentor, or at an online meditation site. Others practice alone. However you do it, working up to meditation for fifteen to twenty minutes before bedtime is enough to guide you into a restful sleep. It's easy and safe—and it's a medication-free alternative. When combined with CBT-I, meditation produces even more effective results. Sources of information about meditation are available at libraries and bookstores and on smartphone apps and YouTube.

The National Sleep Foundation recommends these meditation techniques. Many forms of meditation include elements from all three of them.

- Mindfulness meditation. In this practice, pay attention to your body and become aware of the sound of your breath, the beating of your heart, and the feeling of the floor or the mattress beneath you. Don't let your thoughts wander to your to-do list or tomorrow's big test. If your thoughts go in other directions, steer them back to being aware of your body, and don't judge yourself.
- Concentration meditation. With this form of meditation, you focus your awareness on one specific thing. It could be the sound of rain or the memory of a special day. You might say a mantra—a word, words, or a sound repeated continuously to assist concentration. It could be a wish, such as "I feel sleepy," or a sound such as *Om, Om, Om*, which is a sacred sound and symbol in various Eastern religions.
- Guided meditation. This involves listening to another person (a live instructor or a recording from your library, bookstore, app store, or YouTube, for example) to guide you through your meditation. It may start by asking you to relax your toes, your feet, your legs, and all the way up your body. Instructions lead you through guided imagery in which you imagine a relaxing scene that you enjoy, such as lying on the beach of a lake with waves lapping at the shore.

Try a Little Yoga

Downward dog, cobra, tree pose. Did you know that not all yoga practices involve physical poses such as these? Yoga nidra, for example, uses meditation to help you fall asleep. It doesn't involve any movements or poses. Instead, it focuses on deep breathing to calm your mind and relax your body. Yoga nidra, or yogic sleep, focuses on decreasing anxiety and increasing feelings of relaxation. It can create a state of consciousness somewhere between waking

Regular yoga nidra practice can calm the brain and body to improve sleep. You can take a class or look for a free online video to get started.

and sleeping. Afterward, you may fall asleep more quickly and experience a deeper sleep.

You can find online yoga nidra videos or take a class to get started. Another source is the online site of *Yoga Journal* magazine, which lists ten steps for yoga nidra. Other yoga nidra practices may be slightly different, but the goal and basic techniques are similar.

1. Begin by lying on your back in a comfortable place and position with your head resting on your favorite pillow. It's okay to listen to calming music too.
2. Connect to your heart's dearest desire. Think about what you want more than anything else. Maybe what you want the most at that moment is to sleep.
3. Make a plan for the session. It may be to fall asleep or to relax after a too busy day.
4. Find your inner resource, the safe haven in your body where you feel secure and calm.

5. Know your body. Be aware of every part of it. Imagine your body radiating sensation just as the sun radiates warmth.
6. Become aware of your breathing. Feel it. Hear it.
7. Welcome your feelings without judgment. Try to call up serenity instead of stress.
8. Notice and welcome the thoughts, memories, and images present in your mind.
9. Experience joy spreading from your body into the space around you.
10. Observe yourself. Stop thinking and instead experience awareness.
11. Reflect on the journey you just completed. Slowly return to your waking life, grateful for taking this time for yourself.

During a normal day, the body's temperature rises and falls slightly. At night when you become drowsy, your temperature falls more than usual and reaches its lowest level at about 5:00 a.m. The temperature of your bedroom can affect the way you sleep. If your room is too warm, it might interfere with sleep or make you restless and uncomfortable. According to the National Sleep Foundation, the ideal room temperature for a good night's sleep is 65°F (18°C). If that seems too cool for you, wear warm pajamas and curl up under a soft blanket or two. Wear socks if your feet get cold.

A fan in your bedroom can make the air in your room seem cooler. Whether it's a ceiling fan or a table fan, having air moving in your room may be all you need to feel more comfortable. Most of us sleep better in a quiet environment. A quiet fan can block out any noise that might keep you awake. The regular humming of the fan provides white noise, a continuous background sound that drowns out other noise. A sound machine is even better. These small machines block out other noises and most have several settings. You can pick the one you like best: white noise, a gentle rain shower, or the sound of waves breaking on a beach. Sleep buds can also block noises. Some models emit soothing sounds to help relax you and help you sleep better.

The darker you can make your bedroom, the better. Sleep with your door shut if possible. Heavy curtains or dark window shades can block outside light. Sleep masks block out most light, are comfortable to wear, and come in a wide variety of styles and patterns.

Aromatherapy can help too. Any fragrance that makes you happy can help you sleep better. Studies show that pleasant odors trigger smell receptors in the nose to send calming messages to the nervous system and set the stage for a good sleep. You can use a diffuser or put a few drops of your favorite essential oil on your wrist or on a cloth that you then place underneath your pillow. Sweet dreams, here we come.

A small fan in your bedroom can provide a gentle, rhythmic, and relaxing noise to help you sleep. Sound machines do the same thing, though a fan is a good way to also make the temperature feel cooler.

Here are some helpful scents for sleep:

- Lavender, used for centuries as a calming fragrance, decreases anxiety and agitation. It helps to relax the body and mind, which can improve sleep quality.
- Vanilla is famous for inducing relaxation. In one test, people who smelled vanilla while taking a stress test had lower blood pressure and more stable heart rates than those who took the same test without vanilla fragrance.
- Jasmine, with its sweet-smelling white petals, is an even more powerful sleep aid than lavender. People inhaling the scent of jasmine reported less restlessness while sleeping and a better quality of sleep.
- Valerian, known to help reduce anxiety when taken by mouth, may also help you sleep better. Valerian has a strong, earthy odor, which may not appeal to everyone. When tested on rats, valerian helped them fall asleep faster and sleep longer than rats that didn't sniff valerian.

Bedding for Better Sleep

Ideally, we spend about one-third of our lives sleeping, so a comfortable bed is very important. Some people prefer a soft mattress, others like a firm mattress. Some companies make mattresses that adjust to soft, firm, or in between at the touch of a button. Or a comfortable futon may be just what you need. If possible, pick out sheets in the texture (crisp or soft) and color that you like. You may prefer the look of a neutral color, such as white or cream. Blue, green, yellow, and earth tones are soothing. While flowered sheets can be lovely, they may not be restful and may clash with wallpaper or curtains. Be sure to pick a comfy quilt or spread to go with your sheets.

THIRTEEN HACKS FOR BETTER SLEEP

1. Exercise early in the day. Exercising too close to bedtime may keep you awake.
2. Get fifteen minutes of sunlight each morning to help regulate melatonin. Light turns off melatonin production, while darkness turns it on.
3. Avoid napping during the day.
4. Go to bed at the same time each night.
5. Put your electronic devices to bed an hour before your own bedtime.
6. If you don't fall asleep within half an hour, get out of bed and go in another room. Do something relaxing like reading or taking a warm shower.
7. Always get up at the same time each morning, even on weekends.
8. Make sure your room is dark, quiet, and cool, about 65°F (18°C) for the best sleep.
9. Use your bed only for sleeping—no eating or TV.
10. Listen to quiet music before bed.
11. Try herbal tea or warm milk before bedtime.
12. Avoid eating anything within two to three hours of bedtime. Snacks before bedtime may prevent you from falling asleep.
13. Especially avoid anything with caffeine in it such as chocolate or cocoa.

Pillows may be the most important part of your bedding. Select the one that's right for you: soft or firm, feathers or foam. Special pillows for side sleepers, back sleepers, and stomach sleepers are also available. You might even like a full-length body pillow to hug against your chest. Or get several pillows to curl up with. Do you have a favorite stuffed animal you like? Be sure to bring it to bed with you and cuddle up.

Body pillows are a great way to feel cozy and safe when you sleep. They come in different sizes, and you can even find fun pillow covers for them.

Did you ever notice how newborn babies are swaddled—wrapped tightly in a blanket? This makes them feel more secure and comfortable, and they sleep better. Teens and adults are trying it for themselves with weighted blankets. The most common weight is 15 pounds (6.8 km) to 20 pounds (9 km). The blankets are soft and comfortable, and stuffed with glass and plastic beads for extra weight. While few studies have scientifically tested weighted blankets, people who use them say they work.

One London newspaper found weighted blankets help with sleeping disorders, decrease stress and anxiety, and improve relaxation. Weighted blankets may cost more than regular blankets and can be too warm in some weather. Some brands offer different weight and cooling options in the same blanket. And while some people like the gentle hug of a weighted blanket, others may not.

Prepare Your Brain and Your Body

Certain foods can help you get to sleep more quickly. For example, several kinds of nuts are beneficial. Almonds are high in magnesium, which can help you stay asleep. Walnuts are a good source of tryptophan, a substance that aids sleep. Pistachios help with melatonin production. Dairy products such as cheese, yogurt, and milk also have tryptophan, which helps to trigger melatonin production. Adding honey to a mug of warm chamomile or passionflower tea can help you to relax. Avoid high-calorie, high-sugar snacks at bedtime because they can actually delay the onset of sleep.

SET SLEEP GOALS

Aim for eight to nine hours of sleep each night. If you're not sleeping enough, choose three or four of the following goals for a few months to see if your sleep improves. For best results, try all eight of them!

1. I won't take my phone to bed with me. I'll put it on silent mode or turn it off and leave it across the room.

2. I'll try a cooler temperature in my bedroom.

3. If my bedroom is noisy, I'll use a fan or a sound machine to block the noise.

4. I won't sleep in on the weekend. I'll get up at my usual time.

5. I won't have any caffeine after 1:00 p.m.

6. If I wake up and can't go back to sleep, I'll get out of bed and read or meditate.

7. If my pillow is not comfortable, I'll get a new one.

8. I'll turn off all electronic devices about an hour before I plan to go to bed.

Psychologist and sleep specialist Dr. Michael J. Breus recommends dividing the final hour before bedtime into twenty-minute segments (after turning off your electronic devices) and following the same ritual every night. For the first twenty minutes, complete any unfinished business such as walking the dog or doing a final chore for your parents. During the second twenty minutes, do something relaxing, such as writing in your journal or meditating. And during the final twenty minutes, complete your personal hygiene activities, such as brushing your teeth, washing your face, or taking a warm, soothing shower. A consistent bedtime ritual can prepare your mind and body for a good night's sleep. And once you're in bed, soothing music works for some people, while listening to an audiobook while drifting off will help others.

If you have negative thoughts about sleep, your sleep could suffer. Set realistic expectations. Try to avoid the stress and anxiety that keep you awake. When you don't sleep well one night, take it in stride. One night of poor sleep doesn't mean the next night or the rest of the week will be impacted. So if you can't sleep one night, try to avoid judging yourself.

Experts say that we can control many of the problems we have with sleep. Seek help if you need it. It might be tricky at first, but you can do it! Sleep better. Be healthier. Be happier.

ANSWERS TO QUIZ ON PAGE 47

True. It's hard to keep your grades up if you sleep through part of class.

False. Teens need nine to ten hours of sleep per night.

False. Caffeine stays in your system at least six hours and makes it difficult to fall asleep.

False. Sleeping late on weekends can reset your internal clock making it harder to fall asleep on weeknights.

False. Blue light coming from computer or TV screens suppresses melatonin, the natural hormone that helps you fall asleep.

False. Going to sleep at your usual time the night before a test improves your memory and concentration.

False. The few extra minutes of sleep the snooze alarm gives you is not a deep sleep and may make it even harder to get up.

True. It can also improve relationships and your school performance.

Glossary

biofeedback: a technique to learn how to control bodily functions such as relaxation through the use of various monitors, including devices that measure heart rate, breathing, and brain waves

blue light: part of the visible light spectrum. Electronic devices emit blue light, which delays the release of melatonin and makes it more difficult to fall asleep.

body mass index (BMI): a ratio between a person's height, weight, age, and gender that doctors use to determine whether a person is at a healthy weight, underweight, overweight, or obese

circadian rhythm: the body's twenty-four-hour internal clock that runs in the background of the brain and cycles between sleepiness and alertness at regular intervals; also known as the sleep-wake cycle

cognitive behavioral therapy for insomnia (CBT-I): a structured talk therapy where a person works with a counselor or therapist to identify negative thoughts that may keep them from sleeping. The patient learns to replace those thoughts with habits that promote sleep.

continuous positive airway pressure (CPAP): a machine that blows pressurized air through a face mask to help keep a person's airway open. This is a common and effective treatment for people with sleep apnea.

electroencephalogram (EEG): a test used to evaluate the electrical activity in the brain during sleep. Doctors use it to help diagnose sleep disorders.

Food and Drug Administration (FDA): the US government agency that regulates the safety of both prescription and over-the-counter medications. The FDA does not regulate dietary supplements such as herbal remedies.

gamma-aminobutyric acid (GABA): a chemical the brain produces that helps the nervous system relax, reduces stress and pain, and suppresses activity in parts of the brain that normally arouse or waken us, boosting our drive to sleep

hippocampus: a region of the brain responsible for short-term memory. It also helps to regulate motivation, emotion, and learning.

hypnotics: a class of medications prescribed for sleep. They may help temporarily, but ongoing use carries a variety of risks including dependence. Common brands include Ambien, Lunesta, and Sonata.

insomnia: not getting enough sleep. This disorder is characterized by falling asleep too late at night, waking during the night and not being able to go back to sleep, or waking too early in the morning.

meditation: the practice of relaxing the body and focusing the mind on restful and pleasant thoughts. When practiced regularly, meditation slows the pulse, lowers blood pressure, and decreases stress hormones, all of which make it easier to fall asleep.

melatonin: a chemical produced by the pineal gland in the brain when darkness falls and that helps us sleep. Melatonin production decreases during the daytime, creating a normal state of wakefulness.

microbiome: billions of bacteria, viruses, fungi, and protozoa in the human intestinal tract that help regulate immune system function as well as hormones that regulate sleep. The gut microbiome has its own circadian rhythm that communicates with the brain.

nightmare: a disturbing dream filled with terrifying images that may awaken the sleeper. Nightmares occur during REM sleep later at night and into the morning. People usually remember their nightmares the next day. About four out of ten teens have nightmares.

night terror: an episode in which a child may scream, appear fearful, sit up, or get out of bed. The frightened child is unlikely to awaken or to remember the episode in the morning. Night terrors occur early in the night during non-REM sleep. Most people grow out of them as they get older.

non-REM parasomnia: a state of consciousness between sleep and a waking state. People with this disorder can be awake enough to perform complex behaviors, such as walking, driving, or even harming themselves or others. However, they are not awake enough to be aware of or have responsibility for their actions. Someone with non-REM parasomnia is unlikely to remember what they did.

parasomnia: an abnormal event related to sleep such as sleep paralysis, nightmares, night terrors, and non-REM and REM sleep behavior disorder

pineal gland: a pea-sized organ in the center of the brain that releases melatonin, which helps to regulate sleep

rapid eye movement (REM) sleep: a state of sleep in which the sleeper is often dreaming and the eyes flutter back and forth as if the dreamer were watching a movie playing out on the inside of the closed eyelids

REM sleep behavior disorder: a condition in which a person does not experience the paralysis that normally happens during REM sleep. With this disorder, a person may act out dreams, especially when dreams are intense or violent.

sedative: a class of prescription medication that helps people relax. Sometimes called tranquilizers, these medications can help with sleep but are risky for long-term use because they can lead to dependence and make it more difficult to sleep. They include the brand names Valium and Librium.

sleep apnea: also called obstructive sleep apnea (OSA); a potentially serious disorder, usually due to partial closure of the airway, in which people stop breathing for a short moment many times during the night. A person with sleep apnea may sound as if they are gasping or choking.

sleep paralysis: the temporary inability to move even though the mind and senses are fully awake. This parasomnia is usually caused by a disturbed REM cycle.

sleepwalking: an abnormal behavior associated with sleep in which a sleeping person gets out of bed and moves around without being aware of doing so. It can occur during the stages of non-REM deep sleep as well as while dreaming during REM sleep. Both types of sleepwalking have the potential to cause injury to the sleeping person or others.

stages of sleep: the sleep cycles through which the brain passes when a person is sleeping. Stage 1 is the transition from wakefulness to light sleep within ten minutes of lying down. Heartbeat, breathing, and brain activity begin to slow, and muscle activity decreases. During stage 2, the heart and breathing slow even more, and the entire body relaxes. Brain activity slows even further, and body temperature drops. Stage 3 is the deep sleep the body and mind need to feel refreshed in the morning. It occurs during the first half of the night. Brain waves, breathing, and heartbeat slow down and muscles are very relaxed. These stages lead to REM sleep.

suprachiasmatic nucleus: a small group of nerve cells deep inside the brain where the optic nerves from our eyes meet and cross. It samples the light each optic nerve receives and uses it to calibrate our internal clock.

uvula: the small piece of skin that hangs above the back of the throat that may contribute to obstructive sleep apnea

Source Notes

4   Meggie Royer, "All Human Beings Spend 1/3 of Their Lives Asleep," *Writings for Winter*, March 20, 2013, https://writingsforwinter.tumblr.com/post/45885325772/all-human-beings-spend-13-of-their-lives-asleep.

5   Arianna Huffington, *The Sleep Revolution: Transforming Your Life One Night at a Time* (New York: Harmony Books, 2017), 18.

6   Timothy Morgenthaler, "Insomnia Increases Risk of Motor Vehicle Deaths, Other Fatal Injuries," American Academy of Sleep Medicine press release, October 31, 2014, https://aasm.org/insomnia-increases-risk-of-motor-vehicle-deaths-other-fatal-injuries/.

8   Lucretia King, in Shiriel King Ambramson, *Restless Nights, Droop Days: Insomniacs Reflect on Life without Sleep*, Redwood Bark, November 6, 2014, https://redwoodbark.org/14514/culture/top-culture/restless-nights-droopy-days-insomniacs-reflect-on-life-without-sleep/.

9   Lydia Wytrzes, interview with the author, November 18, 2019.

11   Jesse Smith, interview with the author, July 3, 2019.

12   "Why Electronics May Stimulate You before Bed," National Sleep Foundation, accessed September 28, 2019, https://www.sleepfoundation.org/articles/why-electronics-may-stimulate-you-bed.

7   "How Much Sleep Do We Really Need?," National Sleep Foundation, accessed February 3, 2020, https://www.sleepfoundation.org/articles/how-much-sleep-do-we-really-need.

8   George Foreman, "50 of the Best Sleep Quotes," SensaCalm, posted September 7, 2018, https://www.sensacalm.com/blogs/news/best-sleep-quotes.

13   Susan Wood, poem, May 28, 2019.

14   Susan Wood, interview with the author, September 15, 2019.

14   Wood.

14   Wood.

14   Wood.

15   Wood.

15   Wood.

15   Wood.

16   Wood.

16   Wood.

16   Wood.

17   Wood.

17 Wood.

18 Michel A. Cramer Bornemann, in letter June 9, 2017, to Susan Wood.

18 Wood, interview.

18 Wood.

18 Wood.

19 Matthew Walker, *Why We Sleep* (New York: Scribner, 2017), 108.

22 Jenna Evans, in Christopher Brito, "Woman Dreamed She Swallowed Her Engagement Ring. She Actually Swallowed It in Her Sleep," *CBS News*, September 16, 2019, https://www.cbsnews.com/news/woman-swallowed-engagement-ring-in-sleep-during-dream/.

22 Wytrzes, interview, November 19, 2019.

23 Wytrzes, interview, November 19, 2019.

23 David B. Feldman, in "Do Dreams Really Mean Anything?" *Psychology Today*, January 19, 2018, https://www.psychologytoday.com/us/blog/supersurvivors/201801/do-dreams-really-mean-anything.

23 Feldman.

24 Maggie Stiefvater, in Katrina Niidas Holm, "Q & A with Maggie Stiefvater," *Publishers Weekly*, October 31, 2019, https://www.publishersweekly.com/pw/by-topic/childrens/childrens-authors/article/81615-q-a-with-maggie-stiefvater.html.

24 "The Best Way to Keep a Dream Journal," Lucid Dream Society, accessed March 25, 2020, https://www.luciddreamsociety.com/dream-journal/.

24 Michael Twery, in "The Benefits of Slumber," NIH News in Health, April 2013, https://newsinhealth.nih.gov/2013/04/benefits-slumber.

25 Merrill Mitler, in "The Benefits of Slumber," NIH News in Health, April 2013, https://newsinhealth.nih.gov/2013/04/benefits-slumber.

25 Usain Bolt, in Jordan Schultz, "These Famous Athletes Rely on Sleep for Peak Performance," *Huffington Post*, August 14, 2014, https://www.huffpost.com/entry/these-famous-athletes-rely-on-sleep_n_5659345.

25 "Talking Sleep with Simone Biles," YouTube video, 2:31, posted by Mattress Firm, October 15, 2019, https://www.youtube.com/watch?v=25XpYtcX2G4.

27 Karen Carson, interview with the author, October 20, 2019.

27 Jeri Ferris, interview with the author, November 17, 2019.

27 Matthew Walker, in "Sleep Scientist Warns against Walking through Life 'in an Underslept State,'" NPR, *Fresh Air*, October 16, 2017, https://www.npr.org/templates/transcript/transcript.php?storyId=558058812.

28   "Sleep. Waking Up to Sleep's Role in Weight Control," Chan School of Public Health, Harvard University, accessed March 25, 2020, https://www.hsph.harvard.edu/obesity-prevention-source/obesity -causes/sleep-and-obesity/.

29   Yaqoot Fatima, in Alison Pearce Stevens, "Don't Snooze on Getting Enough Sleep," Science News for Students, accessed February 6, 2020, https://www.sciencenewsforstudents.org/article/getting -enough-sleep-health-bmi-learning.

29   Walker, Why We Sleep, 17.

35   Nikoli Rieger, interview with the author, December 14, 2019.

35   Walker, Why We Sleep, 269.

24   Ernest Hemingway, in "50 of the Best Sleep Quotes," SensaCalm, posted September 7, 2018, https://www.sensacalm.com/blogs/news /best-sleep-quotes.

31   Walker, 68.

33   Douglas B. Kirsch, in Adam Popescu, "How to Get More Sleep Tonight," New York Times, March 25, 2020, https://www.nytimes .com/2020/03/25/style/self-care/sleep-tips-benefits-coronavirus.html.

37   "Teens and Sleep," National Sleep Foundation, accessed January 15, 2020, https://www.sleepfoundation.org/articles/teens-and-sleep.

38   David Anderson, in Katherine Martinelli, "ADHD and Sleep Disorders: Are Kids Getting Misdiagnosed?," Child Mind Institute, accessed March 25, 2020, https://childmind.org/article/adhd-sleep-disorders -misdiagnosed/.

38   David DiSalvo, "Why Getting Too Little Sleep Could Lead to Risky Decision Making," Forbes, September 5, 2017, https://www.forbes .com/sites/daviddisalvo/2017/09/05/why-getting-too-little-sleep -could-lead-to-risky-decision-making/#485d04192b37.

39   Jack Ferris, interview with the author, November 28, 2019.

39   Ferris.

40   John Delaney, interview with the author, December 22, 2019.

40   Carter Delaney, interview with the author, December 22, 2019.

40   Lili Delaney, interview with the author, December 22, 2019.

40   Carter Delaney, interview.

40   John Delaney, interview.

40   Cathy Goldstein, in Jamie Ducharme, "Can You Really Catch Up on Lost Sleep?," Time, March 4, 2019, https://time.com/5541101/how-to -catch-up-on-sleep/.

40–41   "Snoozing More on Weekends Isn't Really the Solution," National Sleep Foundation, accessed March 27, 2020, https://www.sleep.org /articles/catching-up-on-sleep/.

42   Libby Vastano, in Christine Hauser and Isabella Kwai, "California Tells Schools to Start Later, Giving Teenagers More Sleep," *New York Times*, October 14, 2019, https://www.nytimes.com/2019/10/14/us /school-sleep-start.html.

42   Wendy M. Troxel, "Teens Are Driving Drowsy Every Day, and That's Dangerous," RAND blog, March 11, 2018, https://www.rand.org/blog /2018/03/teens-are-driving-drowsy-every-day-and-thats-dangerous .html.

43   Talia Dunietz, "Drowsy Driving in Teens," American Academy of Sleep Medicine, accessed February 5, 2020, http://sleepeducation .org/news/2019/02/05/drowsy-driving-in-teens.

44   Robert L. Steinberg, in Laurie Mason Schroeder, "Woman, 20, Gets Jail for Fatal Drowsy Driving Crash," Allentown (PA) *Morning Call News*, April 28, 2015, https://www.mcall.com/news/breaking/mc -parkland-courtney-quinn-fatal-crash-sentence-20150427-story.html.

46   Dale Carnegie, in "50 of the Best Sleep Quotes," SensaCalm, posted September 7, 2018, https://www.sensacalm.com/blogs/news/best -sleep-quotes.

49   Jennifer Hassan, "A Prisoner in My Own Body: This Is What It's Like to Have Sleep Paralysis," *Washington Post*, January 27, 2018, https:// www.washingtonpost.com/national/health-science/a-prisoner-in-my -own-body-this-is-what-its-like-to-have-sleep-paralysis/2018/01 /26/9e59fae4-d60e-11e7-95bf-df7c19270879_story.html.

50   Dr. Dan Denis in Susan Davis, "Sleep Paralysis: Demon in the Bedroom," *WebMd*, January 4, 2011. https://www.webmd.com/sleep -disorders/features/sleep-paralysis-demon-in-the-bedroom#1. Accessed November 5, 2019.

50–51 Wendy Wright, interview with the author, November 11, 2019.

51   Dr. Clete Kushida in Susan Davis, "Sleep Paralysis: Demon in the Bedroom," WebMd, January 4, 2011. https://www.webmd.com/sleep -disorders/features/sleep-paralysis-demon-in-the-bedroom#1. Accessed November 5, 2019.

52   Liu X et al., "Frequent Nightmares May Increase Risk of Suicide, Self-Harm in Teens," *Journal of Clinical Psychiatry*, June 17, 2019, https://www.healio.com/psychiatry/sleep-disorders/news/online /%7B59e3e4bc-1545-4422-90f9-a58fbdcc178b%7D/frequent -nightmares-may-increase-risk-of-suicide-self-harm-in-teens.

54   Darlena Cunha, in "My Daughter's Night Terrors Are My Nightmares," *Washington Post*, May 13, 2015, https://www.washingtonpost.com /news/parenting/wp/2015/05/13/my-daughters-night-terrors-are-my -nightmares/.

53   Kazuhiko Fukuda, in Nicholas D. Kristaf, "Alien Abduction? Science Calls It Sleep Paralysis," *New York Times*, July 6, 1999, https:// www.nytimes.com/1999/07/06/science/alien-abduction-science -calls-it-sleep-paralysis.html.

54   Suzanne Collins, in Goodreads, accessed March 28, 2020, https://www.goodreads.com/quotes/tag/nightmares.

55   "Scary Movies Cause Nightmares, and 8 Other Myths about Dreams—Busted," *Huffington Post*, last modified April 26, 2017, https://www.huffpost.com/entry/dream-myths-busted_\n_572b aa35e4b0bc9cb04628b3.

55   "Nightmares," Nemours Children's Health System, May 3, 2018, https://www.nemours.org/patientfamily/khlibrary/articles/nightmare.html.

55   Gary Levinson, in "The Frightening Truth about Nightmares," Sharp .com, October 31, 2016, https://www.sharp.com/health-news/the -frightening-truth-about-nightmares.cfm.

57   Mike Birbiglia, in Terry Gross, "Spending the Night with Sleepwalker Mike Birbiglia," NPR, *Fresh Air*, October 18, 2018, https://www.npr .org/transcripts/130644070?storyId=130644070?storyId=130644070.

58   Birbiglia.

58   Wytrzes, interview, December 9, 2019.

59   Wytrzes.

60   Wood, interview.

60   Jesse Mindel, in Cassie Shortsleeve, "9 Types of Parasomnias That Might Explain That Weird Thing You Do When You Sleep," Self.com, June 5, 2019, https://www.self.com/story/9-parasomnias-sleep -disorders?verso=true.

61   Carol Ridenour, interview with the author, May 2019.

61   College student, in W. Chris Winter, *The Sleep Solution: Why Your Sleep Is Broken and How to Fix It* (New York: Berkley, 2017), 232.

62   Wood, interview.

63   Paul G. Mathew, in "Snored to Death: The Symptoms and Dangers of Untreated Sleep Apnea," Harvard Health Blog, February 13, 2017, https://www.health.harvard.edu/blog/snored-to-death-the-symptoms -and-dangers-of-untreated-sleep-apnea-2017021311159.

65   Wytrzes, interview, November 18, 2019.

66   Michelle Perfect, in "Obstructive Sleep Apnea (OSA) Persisting into Teens Can Impact Life Skills," American Academy of Sleep Medicine, June 12, 2012, https://aasm.org/obstructive-sleep-apnea-osa-persisting -into-teens-can-impact-life-skills/.

66   Julia Higginson, "When Teens Have Severe Obstructive Sleep Apnea," Alaska Sleep Education Center, accessed December 16, 2019, https://www.alaskasleep.com/blog/when-teens-have-severe -obstructive-sleep-apnea.

66   Wytrzes, interview, November 18, 2019.

68   Alan Schwartz, in "Do Sleep Trackers Really Work?," Johns Hopkins Medicine, accessed March 29, 2020, https://www.hopkinsmedicine.org/health/wellness-and-prevention/do-sleep-trackers-really-work.

68   Charles Dickens, in Goodreads, accessed March 29, 2020, https://www.goodreads.com/quotes/tag/sleeplessness.

71   "Sleep Awareness Week," National Sleep Foundation, accessed March 29, 2020, https://www.sleepfoundation.org/press-release/sleep-awareness-week-2020.

72   Stacie C., in "7 of the Craziest Sleepwalking Stories You'll Ever Hear," *Women's Health*, June 10, 2015, https://www.womenshealthmag.com/health/a19928134/7-of-the-craziest-sleepwalking-stories-youll-ever-hear/.

72   Walker, *Why We Sleep*, 282.

73   Teresa Carr, "The Problem with Sleeping Pills: Benefits Might Be Smaller and the Risks Greater Than You Expect," *Consumer Reports*, December 12, 2018, https://www.news4jax.com/health/2020/02/06/consumer-reports-the-problem-with-sleeping-pills/.

73   Daniel Buysse, in Carr.

77   Carr, "The Problem with Sleeping Pills."

79   Christine, in "Cognitive Behavioral Therapy for Insomnia," National Sleep Foundation, accessed December 17, 2019, https://www.sleepfoundation.org/articles/cognitive-behavioral-therapy-insomnia.

73   "FDA Adds Boxed Warning for Risk of Serious Injuries Caused by Sleepwalking with Certain Prescription Insomnia Medicines," FDA, April 30, 2019, https://www.fda.gov/drugs/drug-safety-and-availability/fda-adds-boxed-warning-risk-serious-injuries-caused-sleepwalking-certain-prescription-insomnia.

76   Eduard de Bruin, Susan Bogels, Frans Oort, and Anne Marie Meijer, "Efficacy of Cognitive Behavioral Therapy for Insomnia in Adolescents: A Randomized Controlled Trial with Internet Therapy, Group Therapy and a Waiting List Condition," *Sleep 38*, no. 12 (December 1, 2015): 1913–1926, https://www.ncbi.nlm.nih.gov/pmc/articles/PMC4667374/.

77   Leonardo da Vinci, in "50 of the Best Sleep Quotes," SensaCalm, posted September 7, 2018, https://www.sensacalm.com/blogs/news/best-sleep-quotes.

81   "Can't Sleep? How Guided Imagery Can Help You Nod Off," National Sleep Foundation, accessed December 27, 2019, https://www.sleep.org/articles/cant-sleep-guided-imagery-can-help-nod-off/.

82   Benjamin Franklin, in "50 of the Best Sleep Quotes."

Selected Bibliography

American Academy of Sleep Medicine. "Obstructive Sleep Apnea (OSA) Persisting into Teens Can Impact Life Skills." Press release, June 12, 2012. https://aasm.org/obstructive-sleep-apnea-osa-persisting-into-teens-can -impact-life-skills/.

Bauer, Brent. "Is Melatonin a Helpful Sleep Aid?" Mayo Clinic, October 10, 2017. https://www.mayoclinic.org/healthy-lifestyle/adult-health/expert -answers/melatonin-side-effects/faq-20057874.

"Benefits of Slumber." National Institutes of Health, April 2013. https:// newsinhealth.nih.gov/2013/04/benefits-slumber.

"Brain Basics: Understanding Sleep." National Institutes of Health, August 13, 2019. https://www.ninds.nih.gov/Disorders/Patient-Caregiver-Education /Understanding-Sleep.

Breus, Michael J. "How Your Stomach Could Be Impacting Your Sleep." *Psychology Today*, November 30, 2018. https://www.psychologytoday .com/us/blog/sleep-newzzz/201811/how-your-stomach-could-be -impacting-your-sleep.

"Can't Sleep? How Guided Imagery Can Help You Nod Off." Sleep.org. Accessed July 23, 2020. https://www.sleep.org/articles/cant-sleep-guided -imagery-can-help-nod-off/.

"What is the Prevalance of Shift Work Disorder?" National Sleep Foundation. Accessed July 23, 2020. http://sleepdisorders. sleepfoundation.org/chapter-5-circadian-rhythm-sleep-disorders /shift-work-type/prevalence/.

"Cognitive Behavioral Therapy for Insomnia." National Sleep Foundation. Accessed July 23, 2020. Sleepfoundation.org/articles/cognitive-behavioral -therapy-insomnia.

"Data and Statistics." Centers for Disease Control and Prevention, May 2, 2017. https://www.cdc.gov/sleep/data_statistics.html.

Donskoy, Innessa, and Darius Loghmanee. "Insomnia in Adolescence." *Medical Sciences* 6, no. 3 (September 2018): 72. https://www.ncbi.nlm.nih .gov/pmc/articles/PMC6164454/.

"Drowsy Driving." Centers for Disease Control and Prevention, March 21, 2017. https://www.cdc.gov/sleep/about_sleep/drowsy_driving.html.

"Drowsy Driving." National Sleep Foundation. Accessed July 23, 2020. https://www.sleepfoundation.org/professionals/drowsy-driving.

Dunietz, Talia M. "Drowsy Driving in Teens." Sleep Education, February 5, 2019. http://sleepeducation.org/news/2019/02/05/drowsy-driving-in-teens.

"FDA Adds Boxed Warning for Risk of Serious Injuries Caused by Sleepwalking with Certain Prescription Insomnia Medicines." Food and Drug Administration, April 30, 2019. https://www.fda.gov/drugs/drug -safety-and-availability/fda-adds-boxed-warning-risk-serious-injuries -caused-sleepwalking-certain-prescription-insomnia.

Higginson, Julia. "When Teens Have Severe Obstructive Sleep Apnea." Alaska Sleep Education Center, June 6, 2017. https://aasm.org/obstructive -sleep-apnea-osa-persisting-into-teens-can-impact-life-skills/.

"How Much Sleep Do We Really Need?" National Sleep Foundation. Accessed July 23, 2020. https://www.sleepfoundation.org/articles/why -electronics-may-stimulate-you-bed.

"How to Meditate before Bed." Sleep.org. Accessed July 23, 2020. https://www.sleep.org/articles/cant-sleep-guided-imagery-can-help-nod -off/.

Li, Yuanyuan, Yanli Hao, Fang Fan, and Bin Zhang. "The Role of Microbiome in Insomnia, Circadian Disturbance and Depression." *Frontiers in Psychiatry* 9 (2018): 669. https://www.ncbi.nlm.nih.gov/pmc/articles /PMC6290721.

Mathew, Paul. "Snored to Death: The Symptoms and Dangers of Untreated Sleep Apnea." Harvard Health Publishing. Last modified December 20, 2017. https://www.health.harvard.edu/blog/snored-to-death-the -symptoms-and-dangers-of-untreated-sleep-apnea-2017021311159.

"Prevalence of NREM [non-REM] Sleep Arousal Disorders." National Sleep Foundation. Accessed July 23, 2020. http://sleepdisorders. sleepfoundation.org/chapter-6-parasomnias/rapid-eye-movement-sleep -behavior-disorder/prevalence/.

"Sleep Aids and Insomnia." National Sleep Foundation. Accessed July 23, 2020. www.sleepfoundation.org/articles/sleep-aids-and-insomnia.

"Sleep Aids: Understand Over-the-Counter Options." Mayo Clinic, October 18, 2019. https://www.mayoclinic.org/healthy-lifestyle/adult -health/in-depth/sleep-aids/art-20047860.

"Sleep Deprivation and Deficiency." National Institutes of Health. Accessed July 23, 2020. nhlbi.nih.gov/health-topics/sleep-deprivation -and-deficiency.

"Sleep in Middle and High School Students." Centers for Disease Control and Prevention, February 5, 2018. https://www.cdc.gov/features/students -sleep/index.html.

"Sleep Scientist Warns against Walking through Life in an Underslept State." NPR, *Fresh Air*, October 16, 2017. https://www.npr.org/templates /transcript/transcript.php?storyId=558058812.

"Sleep Terrors." Mayo Clinic. Accessed July 23, 2020. https://www .mayoclinic.org/diseases-conditions/sleep-terrors/symptoms-causes /syc-20353524.

"Spending the Night with Sleepwalker Mike Birbiglia." NPR, *Fresh Air*, October 18, 2010. https://www.npr.org/transcripts/130644070?storyId=13 0644070?storyId=130644070.

"Students See Improvements with Later School Start Times." American Academy of Sleep Medicine, July 5, 2010. http://sleepeducation.org /news/2010/07/06/students-see-improvements-with-later-school-start -times.

"Teens and Sleep." National Institutes of Health, August 8, 2019. https:// www.ninds.nih.gov/Disorders/Patient-Caregiver-Education/Understanding -Sleep.

"Teens and Sleep." National Sleep Foundation. Accessed July 23, 2020. https://www.sleepfoundation.org/articles/teens-and-sleep.

"Tips for Better Sleep." Centers for Disease Control and Prevention, July 15, 2016. https://www.cdc.gov/sleep/about_sleep/sleep_hygiene.html.

"Why Electronics May Stimulate You before Bed." National Sleep Foundation. Accessed July 23, 2020. www.sleepfoundation.org/articles /why-electronics-may-stimulate-you-bed.

"Youth Risk Behavior Surveillance System." Centers for Disease Control and Prevention, August 22, 2018. https://www.cdc.gov/healthyyouth/data /yrbs/index.htm.

Further Information

Books

Battistin, Jennie Marie. *Mindfulness for Teens in 10 Minutes a Day: Exercises to Feel Calm, Stay Focused & Be Your Best Self.* Emeryville, CA: Rockridge, 2019.

This book will help readers regain control of their sleep and of life through simple and effective exercises that fit perfectly into the daily routine. Learn mindfulness through sixty guided exercises.

Carney, Colleen. *Goodnight Mind for Teens: Skills to Help You Quiet Noisy Thoughts and Get the Sleep You Need.* Oakland: New Harbinger, 2020.

Teens have so many reasons for having trouble sleeping, such as too early school start times, too much late-night screen time, and general anxiety about their future. This book offers tips based on cognitive behavioral therapy to help teens sleep at night and to feel better in the daytime.

Carney, Colleen, and Rachel Manber. *Goodnight Mind: Turn Off Your Noisy Thoughts and Get a Good Night's Sleep.* Oakland: New Harbinger, 2013.

The most common complaint by those who have trouble sleeping is having a "noisy mind." Written by two psychologists who specialize in sleep disorders, the book contains information about insomnia and exercises to better manage pesky bedtime thoughts.

Hirshkowitz, Max, and Patricia B. Smith. *Sleep Disorders for Dummies.* Hoboken, NJ: Wiley, 2004.

This older book does a nice job of covering the basics of insomnia and sleep disorders in an easy-to-read manner appropriate for teen readers. Learn how to prevent and manage sleep disorders, improve sleep habits, and enhance the quality of sleep.

Huffington, Arianna. *The Sleep Revolution.* New York: Harmony, 2017.

Primarily for adult readers, this book acknowledges the sleep deprivation crisis. The author reviews sleep disorders and dreams and discusses proven and unproven methods to achieve better sleep. One chapter covers sleep history and how events such as the Industrial Revolution permanently changed much of humankind's sleep patterns.

Pierce, Simon. *Sleep Disorders: What Keeps People Up at Night?* New York: Lucent, 2019.

Much about sleep remains a mystery, making it difficult to understand and treat sleep disorders and insomnia. Besides useful text, quotes, charts, and sidebars, the book provides a list of organizations to contact for further resources for readers wishing to learn more about a particular disorder they or a family member may be living with.

Stewart, Whitney. *Mindfulness and Meditation: Handling Life with a Calm and Focused Mind.* Minneapolis: Twenty-First Century Books, 2019.
This book introduces readers to the practice of mindfulness. Mindfulness is focusing attention on the present moment. It can change a person's approach to stress, develop skills to handle anxiety and depression, and provide a sense of awareness and belonging. The book provides specific exercises for examining emotions, managing stress, checking social media habits, and setting intentions to increase happiness.

Thompkins, Michael, and Monique Thompson. *The Insomnia Workbook for Teens.* Oakland: New Harbinger, 2018.
This is one of the few books about sleep published specifically for teens. Between changes in circadian rhythm, early school start times, social media, electronic devices, extracurricular activities, and late-night homework, teens are at the highest risk of any age group for sleep deprivation. The workbook offers a wealth of information for teen insomnia and practical methods to get a better night's sleep.

Walker, Matthew. *Why We Sleep: Unlocking the Power of Sleep and Dreams.* New York: Simon and Schuster, 2017.
Walker, a neuroscientist and sleep expert, explains the vital importance of sleep and dreaming. Sleep enriches the ability to learn, memorize, and make logical decisions; it recalibrates emotions; replenishes the immune system; fine-tunes the body's metabolism; and regulates appetite. Dreaming helps to mitigate painful memories.

Winter, W. Chris. *The Sleep Solution.* New York: Berkley, 2018.
Winter, a sleep medicine specialist, covers the basics of sleep and the dangers of not getting enough. He also touches on a number of sleep disorders and makes recommendations for better sleep. The contents include information on understanding how sleep works, learning about insomnia and sleep apnea, and learning how to sleep without sleeping pills.

Websites and Organizations

American Alliance for Healthy Sleep
http://sleepeducation.org/patient-support
This is a patient-focused organization that provides support services and advocacy for patients with all sleep disorders and helps to improve the lives of those patients. Sleep specialists and patients work together to offer helpful programs to those with sleep

problems. The American Academy of Sleep Medicine founded the alliance in 2017.

Center for Disease Control and Prevention (CDC)
https://www.cdc.gov/sleep/about_us.html
The CDC works to improve the health of all Americans in many areas, including sleep. Its mission regarding sleep is to raise the public's awareness about how the problems of insufficient sleep and sleep disorders can affect anyone's health.

Healthline: "17 Proven Tips to Sleep Better at Night"
https://www.healthline.com/nutrition/17-tips-to-sleep-better
This long article has excellent suggestions on how to easily improve your sleeping patterns.

Mayo Clinic
https://www.mayoclinic.org
The Mayo Clinic, a large nonprofit health-care organization based in Rochester, Minnesota; Jacksonville, Florida; and Scottsdale, Arizona, provides hands-on health care, education, and research. Search for articles about sleep. There are dozens of topics, ranging from ways to sleep better, sleep-tracking devices, insomnia, and other sleep disorders. They cover the basics about sleeping better and how important it is.

National Sleep Foundation
https://www.sleepfoundation.org/
The National Sleep Foundation has been an expert for nearly thirty years on sleep. It publishes an annual Sleep in America poll that looks at different aspects of sleep each year. For example, the 2020 poll covered sleepiness in general and found that insomnia affects nearly every aspect of life, including activities, mood, and alertness.

Sleep Education
http://sleepeducation.org/
This website, sponsored by the American Academy of Sleep Medicine, offers dozens of excellent articles about sleep, including insomnia, sleep apnea, jet lag, shift work, snoring, CPAP machines, and healthy sleep habits. The site provides information to help people find qualified sleep testing centers and explains how sleep studies work.

Audio, Movies, and Videos

American Sleep Apnea Association
https://www.sleepapnea.org/learn/sleep-apnea/personal-sleep -apnea-stories/
Listen to a twenty-six-second audio recording of a man with severe sleep apnea.

Center for Human Sleep Science
https://www.humansleepscience.com/m-e-d-i-a-1
This is an eclectic collection of excellent videos about many aspects of sleeping from producers such as the Smithsonian Institution, CBS, and National Public Radio.

"The Mystery of Sleep: Why a Good Night's Rest Is Vital." YouTube video, 57:07. Posted by Talks at Google, April 18, 2017. https://www.youtube.com/watch?v=3oXHIgCAdhQ.
Sleep expert Meir Kryger talks about his 2017 book *The Mystery of Sleep: Why a Good Night's Rest Is Vital*. This video includes discussions of sleep, insomnia, and other sleep disorders. It also offers information about how to improve sleep.

"Om Mantra Chants + 1111 times." YouTube video, 6:56:23. Posted by Meditative Mind, July 5, 2017. https://www.youtube.com/watch?v=sG8NDw3Tv6c.
This combination video and audio recording features hours of continuous Om chanting. According to the site, Om is the inner sound of the cosmos, and it reverberates across the universe, bringing beauty to every cell of the body. Chanting Om is part of some meditation practices. It could be used as a relaxation technique and a gateway to sleep.

Pollan, Michael. Caffeine: *How Caffeine Created the Modern World*. Audible Original, Newark, New Jersey, 2020.
This audiobook finds that caffeine is the most used drug in the world, and the only one routinely given to children. Within a century of being discovered in East Africa, caffeine became an addiction for much of the human species, as the world drinks about two billion cups of coffee each day.

"Sleep Is Your Super Power: Matt Walker." YouTube video, 19:18. Posted by TED, June 3, 2019. https://www.youtube.com/watch?v=5MuIMqhT8DM.
In this TED talk, sleep expert Walker shares what happens to the brain and body when you get enough good sleep and what happens when you don't.

"10 Hours of Deep Sleep Music—Relaxing Music for Sleeping & Meditation by Soothing Relaxation." YouTube video, 10:10:17. Posted by Soothing Relaxation, April 30, 2019. https://www.youtube.com/watch?v=rulvcTfez5w.
This audio channel offers ten hours of relaxing music for meditation before you sleep.

Index

About the Author

Connie Goldsmith has written twenty-five nonfiction books for middle grade and young adult readers and has published more than two hundred magazine articles for adults and children. Her books include *Kiyo Sato: From a WWII Japanese Internment Camp to a Life of Service*; *Women in the Military: From Drill Sergeants to Fighter Pilots* (named a 2020 Bank Street Best Children's Book of the Year); *Pandemic: How Climate, the Environment, and Superbugs Increase the Risk*; *Animals Go to War: From Dogs to Dolphins*; *The Ebola Epidemic: The Fight, the Future* (a Junior

Library Guild selection and Kirkus starred review); and *Bombs over Bikini: The World's First Nuclear Disaster* (a Junior Library Guild Selection, a Children's Book Committee at Bank Street College Best Children's Book of the Year, and an SCBWI Crystal Kite winner).

Goldsmith is a member of the Society of Children's Book Writers and Illustrators and a member of the Authors Guild. She is a registered nurse with a bachelor of science degree in nursing and a master of public administration degree in health care. When she's not writing, she visits with friends and family, pounds out the miles on her treadmill, plays with her crazy cats, and hikes along the American River near Sacramento, California, where she lives.

photo credit: Alan Bradley

Photo Acknowledgments

Image credits: Laura Westlund/Independent Picture Service, pp. 7, 26, 30, 32, 35, 45; fizkes/Shutterstock.com, pp. 10, 84; AP Photo/dpa/picture-alliance, p. 23; AP Photo/Kyodo, p. 25; eggeegg/Shutterstock.com, p. 43; Wikimedia Commons (Public Domain), pp. 53, 60; vasara/Shutterstock.com, p. 67; JPC-PROD/Shutterstock.com, p. 69; ben bryant/Shutterstock.com, p. 86; LarsZ/Shutterstock.com, p. 89.